High Level Models and Methodologies for Information Systems

Pedro Isaias · Tomayess Issa

High Level Models and Methodologies for Information Systems

 Springer

Pedro Isaias
Universidade Aberta
Lisbon
Portugal

Tomayess Issa
School of Information Systems
Curtin University
Perth, WA
Australia

ISBN 978-1-4614-9253-5   ISBN 978-1-4614-9254-2 (eBook)
DOI 10.1007/978-1-4614-9254-2

Library of Congress Control Number: 2014949355

Springer New York Heidelberg Dordrecht London

© Springer Science+Business Media New York 2015
This work is subject to copyright. All rights are reserved by the Publisher, whether the whole or part of the material is concerned, specifically the rights of translation, reprinting, reuse of illustrations, recitation, broadcasting, reproduction on microfilms or in any other physical way, and transmission or information storage and retrieval, electronic adaptation, computer software, or by similar or dissimilar methodology now known or hereafter developed. Exempted from this legal reservation are brief excerpts in connection with reviews or scholarly analysis or material supplied specifically for the purpose of being entered and executed on a computer system, for exclusive use by the purchaser of the work. Duplication of this publication or parts thereof is permitted only under the provisions of the Copyright Law of the Publisher's location, in its current version, and permission for use must always be obtained from Springer. Permissions for use may be obtained through RightsLink at the Copyright Clearance Center. Violations are liable to prosecution under the respective Copyright Law.
The use of general descriptive names, registered names, trademarks, service marks, etc. in this publication does not imply, even in the absence of a specific statement, that such names are exempt from the relevant protective laws and regulations and therefore free for general use.
While the advice and information in this book are believed to be true and accurate at the date of publication, neither the authors nor the editors nor the publisher can accept any legal responsibility for any errors or omissions that may be made. The publisher makes no warranty, express or implied, with respect to the material contained herein.

Printed on acid-free paper

Springer is part of Springer Science+Business Media (www.springer.com)

Preface

This book is both timely and timeless. It is timely in that information systems (IS)—in all their guises—are even more fundamental to business, organizations and society now than ever before. They underpin e-business and social media as well as driving the operations of organizations of all sizes. It is timeless in that we seem to continue to make many of the same mistakes again and again when delivering IS. The better we can understand the past of models and methods for delivering successful IS, hopefully, the less we will repeat those mistakes. We have seen a worrying shift towards strategy in the role for IS. They are clearly strategic, but they must be developed, deployed and they must deliver. But we must also focus on the systems themselves.

There are tensions between used and useful systems. We need to understand better why some systems get used and others do not. We also need to appreciate the role of context and the appropriateness of different development methods. As the context in which the system is, or will be used, changes, so the systems need to change too—and changed more frequently as well as being used by different people for different purposes. All IS development tends to follows a lifecycle. Sometimes this is all planned in advance and sometimes it is incremental. Developers must match process to problem and to requirements. They must also plan for, and deliver, benefits.

In the mid-1990s, I was part of a team at Warwick Business School that developed a 3-D model of Information Systems Success (Ballantine et al. 1996). This model attempted to understand IS success by separating it into three levels; *technical development, deployment* to the user, and *delivery* of business benefits. The model is described later in this book, but it is useful just to reprise it, here in the foreword, as it attempts to uncover the quantity and complexity of the variables that need to be combined in some way so as to allow organizations to derive benefits from their IS.

In the model, *filters act between the levels* of IS effectiveness and inhibit or encourage adoption of the system at the next level, but the filters act independently of the quality of the system at lower levels. *Influencing factors* collectively determine the quality of the information system within levels. Some factors may work at more than one level and not all factors have to be positive in order to achieve a positive result overall. There may be inter-relationships between factors within and across levels. Influencing factors can be endogenous, within the control of actors at the respective levels or exogenous, lying outside such control.

At the *development level*, success is influenced by endogenous factors such as complexity, project management, technology, development method, user involvement, professional skills and experience, and data quality. Output from this level is a technical system that enters the *implementation filter*. Exogenous factors influence implementation that results in the acceptance, or not, of the technical system. A technically excellent system, but one in which users had not participated, might be rejected, as might an imposed system or one that offers nothing that existing systems do not already deliver. An IS can be a success at the development level, but not at the deployment level. Yet, a low quality technical system may be successfully deployed due to the support of a champion, business imperative or management dictate.

A successful, implemented system enters the *deployment level* where factors influence how much, and how well, the system is used. The user is central, as the technical system serves the user and delivers benefits. Deployment success is influenced by user satisfaction, support, information quality, user skills, the resources deployed for implementation and the nature of the task. An IS, although successfully used, may fail to deliver business objectives. The *integration filter* determines whether the system actually works within the organization. It may be prevented from doing so by an organizational structure or politics.

At the *delivery level* forces such as active senior management support, change management skills and benefits management improve fit between the system and the organization. The resources available and the way output from the system is used affect success, as does the alignment of individual and business objectives. However, even achieving business objectives may not result in increased business performance, due to exogenous factors in the *environment filter*. These include competitor movements and political, social, and economic factors.

The primary purpose of outlining this model here is to communicate that IS success is not simple. We need to draw a wide boundary around the notion of the information system and appreciate the rich and complex scope and impact of IS. This book attempts to do this. It is a source guide to the theory and practice of IS methods and methodologies. But crucially it offers a multi-disciplinary approach to these, allied to a depth of understanding. It is contemporary—as system use changes so do methods to deliver them. And it is clear about the need to understand context. It is a book that will appeal to students of IS, to those researching in IS, and to those whose main role is to develop IS. Hopefully, it will help us to avoid repeating the mistakes of the past and to deliver more useful, used systems.

Birkbeck, University of London, UK   Philip Powell

Reference

Ballantine, J., Bonner, M., Levy, M., Martin, A., Munro, I., & Powell, P. (1996). The 3-D model of information systems success: The search for the dependent variable continues. *Information Resources Management Journal,* 9(4), 5–14.

Acknowledgments

We acknowledge the support of all people that contributed directly or indirectly to this book.

The first author would like to thank in general Paula Miranda and Ana Avelans for their on-going support and more specifically to (in alphabetical order) Liliana Silva, Marta O. Martins, Sandra S. Santos, and Sara S. Pífano. Finally, he would like to acknowledge the support of his family. Without their assistance, this work would not be possible at all.

The second author owes special gratitude first to almighty and her family for their continuous support, and encouragement since without their help, this work would never have been completed.

Lisbon, Portugal   Pedro Isaias
Perth, WA, Australia   Tomayess Issa

Contents

**1 Introduction to Information Systems Models
and Methodologies** 1
   1.1   Introduction 1
   1.2   Systems Development Paradigms 2
   1.3   IS Development Life cycles 4
   1.4   IS Development Methodologies 6
   1.5   Web Site Development Methodologies 9
   1.6   Usability Evaluation Models 11
   1.7   Quality Evaluation Models 13
   1.8   IS Models for Success Assessment 14
   1.9   Conclusions 16
   References 17

2 Information System Development Life Cycle Models 21
   2.1   Introduction 21
   2.2   The Waterfall Model 22
   2.3   The Incremental Model 24
   2.4   The Spiral Life Cycle Model 26
   2.5   The V Life Cycle Model 28
   2.6   Rapid Application Development 29
   2.7   Agile Life Cycle Model 31
   2.8   The Prototyping Model 33
   2.9   Usability Engineering Life Cycle 35
   2.10   The Star Life Cycle Model 35
   2.11   Hybrid System Development Life Cycles 37
   2.12   Conclusion 38
   References 38

3 Information Systems Development Methodologies ... 41
- 3.1 Introduction ... 41
- 3.2 Information Systems Development Methodologies ... 42
  - 3.2.1 Agile Methodology ... 42
  - 3.2.2 Structured Systems Analysis and Design Methodology (SSADM) ... 43
  - 3.2.3 Soft Systems Methodology (SSM) ... 45
  - 3.2.4 User-centered Development Methodology ... 47
  - 3.2.5 ETHICS Methodology ... 49
  - 3.2.6 STRADIS Methodology ... 51
  - 3.2.7 Information Engineering (IE) ... 52
  - 3.2.8 Jackson Systems Development (JSD) ... 53
  - 3.2.9 Information Systems Work and Analysis of Changes (ISAC) ... 55
  - 3.2.10 Multiview Methodology ... 56
- 3.3 Conclusion ... 57
- References ... 58

4 Web Site Development Methodologies ... 63
- 4.1 Introduction ... 63
- 4.2 The W3DT Methodology ... 63
- 4.3 The Web Site Design Method ... 65
- 4.4 Relationship Management Methodology (RMM) ... 66
- 4.5 Object-Oriented Hypermedia Design Methodology (OOHDM) ... 68
- 4.6 Web Engineering ... 70
- 4.7 Internet Commerce Development Methodology (ICDM) ... 72
- 4.8 Web Information System Development Methodology (WISDM) ... 74
- 4.9 Participative Methodology for Developing Web Sites ... 76
- 4.10 Conclusion ... 79
- References ... 80

5 Usability Evaluation Models ... 83
- 5.1 Introduction ... 83
- 5.2 Cognitive Engineering ... 83
- 5.3 Cognitive Walk-throughs ... 84
- 5.4 Heuristic Evaluation ... 85
- 5.5 Goals, Operators, Methods, and Selection Rules (GOMS) ... 86
- 5.6 Executive Process-Interactive Control (EPIC) Model ... 87
- 5.7 Adaptative Control of Thought-Rational Model ... 88
- 5.8 Adaptative Control of Thought in Information Foraging Model (Act-IF) ... 88
- References ... 89

6 Quality Evaluation Models ... 91
- 6.1 Introduction ... 91
- 6.2 Technology Acceptance Model (TAM) ... 92
- 6.3 Technology Acceptance Model 2 (TAM2) ... 95
- 6.4 The Web of System Performance (WOSP) ... 97
- 6.5 Theory of Reasoned Action (TRA) ... 100
- 6.6 Theory of Planned Behavior (TPB) ... 102
- 6.7 Task–Technology Fit Model (TTF) ... 104
- 6.8 Innovation Diffusion Theory (IDT) ... 107
- 6.9 Expectation–Disconfirmation Theory (EDT) ... 109
- 6.10 Expectation–Confirmation Model of IS Continuance ... 111
- 6.11 The Social Influence Model ... 112
- 6.12 Unified Theory of Acceptance and Use of Technology (UTAUT) ... 114
- 6.13 Conclusion ... 116
- References ... 117

7 Information Systems' Models for Success Assessment ... 121
- 7.1 Introduction ... 121
- 7.2 Delone and McLean's IS Success Model ... 122
- 7.3 Seddon Model ... 126
- 7.4 3D Model of Information Systems Success ... 130
- 7.5 IS-impact Measurement Model ... 132
- 7.6 Strategic Information Systems Planning (SISP) Effectiveness ... 134
- 7.7 Other Models for IS Success Evaluation ... 138
- 7.8 Conclusions ... 139
- References ... 139

Index ... 141

About the Authors

Dr. Pedro Isaias (Universidade Aberta, Portugal, pisaias@uab.pt) is an associate professor at Universidade Aberta (Portuguese Open University) in Lisbon, Portugal, responsible for several courses and director of the master degree program in Electronic Commerce and Internet since its start in 2003 until 2014. He is currently director for the Master of Science and MBA in Management. He is co-founder and president of IADIS—International Association for Development of the Information Society, a scientific non-profit association. He holds a Ph.D. in Information Management (in the speciality of information and decision systems) from the New University of Lisbon. Author of several books (both as author/co-author and editor/co-editor), journal and conference papers, and research reports, all in the information systems area, he has headed several conferences and workshops within the mentioned area. He has also been responsible for the scientific coordination of several EU funded research projects. He is co-editor of the Interactive Technologies and Smart Education (ITSE) Journal, the editor of the IADIS Journal on WWW/Internet (IJWI) and the co-editor of the IADIS Journal on Computer Science and Information Systems (IJCSIS). He is also member of the editorial board of several journals and program committee member of several conferences and workshops. At the moment he conducts research activity related to Information Systems in general, E-Learning, E-Commerce and WWW related areas.

Dr. Tomayess Issa is a senior lecturer at the School of Information Systems at Curtin University, Australia. Tomayess completed her doctoral research in Web Development and Human Factors. As an academic, she is also interested in establishing teaching methods and styles to enhance the students' learning experiences and resolve problems that students face. Tomayess Issa is a Conference and Program Co-Chair of the IADIS International Conference on Internet Technologies and Society and IADIS International Conference on International Higher Education.

Furthermore she initiated the IADIS conference for Sustainability, Green IT and Education. Currently, she conducts research locally and globally in information systems, Human–Computer Interaction, Usability, Social Networking, Sustainability, Green IT, Cloud Computing and Teaching and Learning.

Tomayess participated in a couple of conferences and published her work in several peer-reviewed journals, books, book chapters, papers and research reports. Tomayess Issa is a Project leader in the International Research Network (IRNet-EU (Jan 2014–2016)) for study and development of new tools and methods for advanced pedagogical science in the field of ICT instruments, e-learning and intercultural competences.

Chapter 1
Introduction to Information Systems Models and Methodologies

1.1 Introduction

As information technology (IT) permeates more and more aspects of human life, information systems (IS) have grown to become an essential component of organizational management. Iivari and Hirschheim (1996) define an information system as a system providing users with information on specified topics within an organizational context, with computers as its main support. Alter (2008), on the other hand, defines an information system as a work system whose activities are centered on the processing of information. IS ultimately provide the support for an organization's networks of information creation, gathering, processing, or storing.

Today, a solid IS, one that is generally accepted by its users and proves to be successful, can determine the success of a business, in a world where competition is ever fiercer. Accordingly with this phenomenon, researchers have grown more and more interested in establishing IS development methodologies and models that can be used across a wide range of contexts, with the purpose of finding ordered, systemic frameworks among the immense variety of techniques and methods that can be found in practice. On the other hand, as IS become more complex, there is a growing need for organizations to have a basis of logical constructs that can provide them with the tools to easily define, control, and integrate all the components of the system (Zachman 1987).

The great variety of existing models for IS development is rooted in the fact that developers of a system will be guided by a number of influences related not only with the object of their work (the goal of the system they are developing), but also with the very nature of their organization, and how it affects expectations. As the developer absorbs these influences, so does the system being built (Hirschheim and Klein 1989), leading to a large number of possible variables, which in turn complicates bringing out a unified view of the problem.

Research has not only focused on the creation and development of IS, but also on what happens to the system beyond its implementation stage, particularly regarding its acceptance or not within the context of the organization and the user base. The interest in defining what can "make or break" a new system has also lead researchers to focus on building models that can help an organization or project manager determine and measure the system's success.

In this book, we will discuss the major methodologies that have been established in existing literature related to systems development and acceptance, as well as the more prominent models that are rooted in each methodological approach. This will allow us to identify how specific methodologies and models are fit for specific types of IS development projects, underlining the usefulness of such theoretical frameworks for practitioners that want to identify which methods are best for their specific projects.

This book is organized into the following chapters:

Chapter 1—Introduction to IS Models and Methodologies (the current chapter);
Chapter 2—IS Development Life Cycle Models;
Chapter 3—IS Development Methodologies;
Chapter 4—Web Site Development Methodologies;
Chapter 5—Usability Evaluation Models;
Chapter 6—Quality Evaluation Models;
Chapter 7—IS Models for Success Assessment.

Each of the chapters, from 2 to 7, will be briefly introduced in the next pages of this Chap. 1 and detailed in the remaining book.

1.2 Systems Development Paradigms

The vast body of research that relates to IS development has led some researchers to attempt to group different methods into a set of simple categories, based on common principles and similarities. These categories, or paradigms, are essentially formed by the underlying philosophies, goals, guiding principles, and fundamental concepts that justify the choice of a given approach to IS development (Iivari et al. 1998).

According to the seminal work of Hirschheim and Klein (1989), there are four paradigms of IS development, which, in turn, are based on paradigms of systems analysis (see Fig. 1.1).

The *functionalist paradigm* focuses on the context, social order, consensus, needs, and rational choices. IS are developed by application of formal concepts, through methodical and planned intervention and based on rational principles. The *social relativist paradigm* focuses on individual subjectivity and the personal frame of reference of the social actor. IS development takes into account the subjective and cultural context of the developer. The *radical structuralist paradigm* advocates the need to transcend existing limitations born out of social and organizational structures. IS development is built by an awareness of necessities and limits and what can be done to improve the system beyond that border. Finally, the

1.2 Systems Development Paradigms

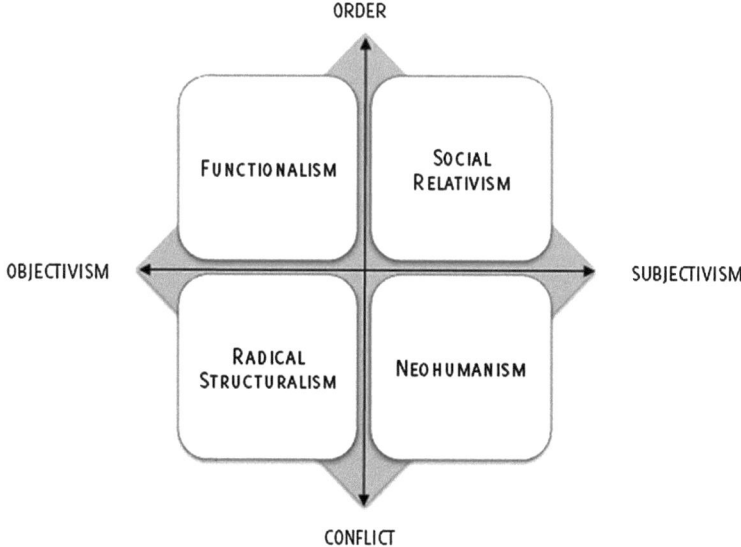

Fig. 1.1 Four paradigms of IS development (adapted from Hirschheim and Klein 1989)

neohumanist paradigm emphasizes the role of different social and organizational forces in exercising change. IS development is shaped by the rationality of human action (Hirschheim and Klein 1989).

Iivari and Hirschheim (1996) build on this concept to define three major aspects that shape the modeling of IS and can be used to determine different underlying paradigms: the organizational context and user base (host organization), the topic of interest to the users (universe of discourse), and computers (technology). They are common across the board of IS methodologies; however, there is great variety in how each information system is conceived at each level (Iivari and Hirschheim 1996). An approach that focuses on the technical level, for example, will have its emphasis placed on methodic planning and design, and prototyping.

Iivari et al. (1998) eventually expanded the four paradigms into a set of new five approaches. The *interactionist approach* focuses on the social use of IS and defines IS as institutions, with complex and overlapping interactions and negotiations between actors. The *speech act-based approach* focuses on communications and communicative action and perceives the IS as a communication system that mediates speech acts or a formalization of professional language. The *soft systems methodology approach* focuses on the learning methodology and the IS as a support system for human activity. The *trade unionist approach* focuses on the worker and perceives computers as tools, and IS as support systems for working relationships, built with collective participation. The *professional work practice approach* aims at combining performance and management principles and perceives that IS development requires a balance between methodological and practical approaches (Iivari et al. 1998).

The discussion of paradigms and approaches is important because it allows to determine a broader context for different IS development practices and provides them with a position within the frameworks of systems analysis and general social sciences. On the other hand, this also allows for a better understanding of how principles of general scientific paradigms can improve systems development (Iivari et al. 1998).

Paradigms established through research are intimately connected with systems development in practice. A paradigm does not constitute a methodology for practical interpretation. However, existing examples in practice are the fundamental drive behind the definition and further research of these paradigms. An existing system becomes part of a body of knowledge that can further fuel the body of research. But that system can also gain from the existing body of research, by adopting certain of its principles. Therefore, for some authors, systems development provides researchers with the necessary component of experience that can further the advancement of research (Nunamaker et al. 1991). Thus, it can be asserted that paradigms are useful tools that can aid in the process of systems development, by providing simple frameworks that can be identified with the organization's culture and goals.

1.3 IS Development Life Cycles

A system development life cycle (SDLC) is a framework oriented toward the description of the sequence of activities or stages that a given product goes through between its conception and its implementation or acceptance. Generally, all projects go through these stages, but there are numerous different models of SDLC that are more or less appropriate to particular types of project. The developers have to pinpoint the characteristics of their project and figure which of the SDLC models is more useful for their situation (Massey and Satao 2012).

The concept of SDLC emerged as a framework for software development in the late 1960s, particularly oriented toward large-scale developments under traditional methodologies. However, it has since then evolved to become a general concept for systems development of any kind, including IS (Patterson 2004). Some life cycle models have also attempted to break from the rigid structure of initial concepts and approach the more flexible agile methodology.

SDLC can be divided into two generic types. First, there are the waterfall-type models, thus named due to the seminal work of Royce (1970) who outlined an SDLC model of successive stages sequenced downward like the flow of a waterfall (see Fig. 1.2). This model essentially presented the ideal strategy for a development project, by outlining some principles of good practices, such as design before coding, rigorous documentation of each stage, and appropriate planning (Munassar and Govardhan 2010). It described the development project in a sequence that can be summarized in five steps: analysis, design, coding, testing, and implementation (Balaji and Murugaiyan 2012). It is, essentially, a description of a product's

1.3 IS Development Life Cycles

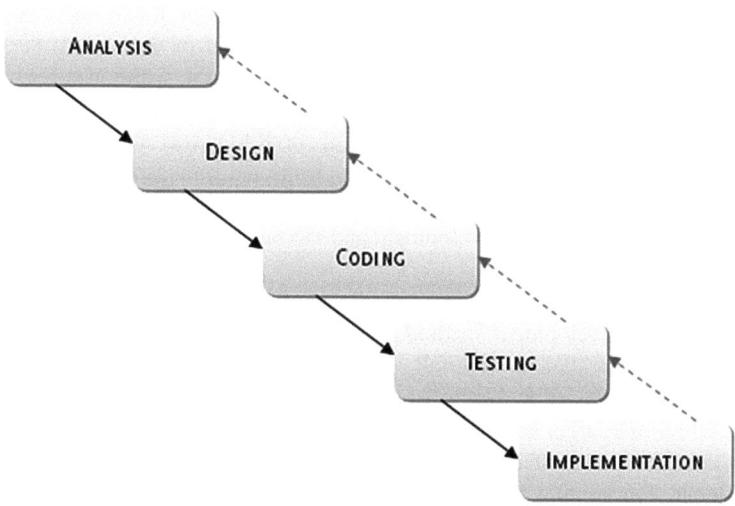

Fig. 1.2 Waterfall model (adapted from Balaji and Murugaiyan 2012)

development under the perspective of traditional methodologies, with an emphasis on the process, rigorous documentation, and self-contained stages. It was the first approach to SDLC in research.

The second type of SDLC comprises the incremental-type models. The incremental model contradicts the waterfall principle of developing a system in a single-pass process, with rigorous documentation and an extensive testing stage, to produce a final, fully usable product in the end. Incremental models instead propose developing a system in successive builds or increments. With each build, the system is designed and developed, and a working version or prototype is implemented. Users can then test it actively, within working contexts, and provide valuable feedback. This feedback will then be used as a starting point for the next build. With each successive build, the system becomes more complete, more functional, and closer to what the users intend (Massey and Satao 2012).

Most models of SDLC can be considered variants of the waterfall model, the increment model, or a combination of both. By introducing innovative concepts within the structure of the original models, or by bringing together the strong points of each one, researchers have attempted to build ideal models of SDLC for many years, resulting in a great variety of different approaches.

The V-model was an adaptation of the waterfall model that attempted to emphasize the testing stage, by proposing that each stage of the process entails a certain type of testing activity. It was presented in the shape of a V. The first sequence of events moves downward like the waterfall model, from analysis of requirements, to high- and low-level design, and coding. Once coding is complete, and a new sequence of actions moves upward, comprising all the different testing phases that should be followed: unit testing, integration testing, system testing, and acceptance testing (Balaji and Murugaiyan 2012).

The spiral SDLC model (Boehm 1988) proposed a much more complex approach to the incremental model, where development of the system is built in successive waves, much like the growing arms of a spiral, while also introducing the concept of risk analysis in the process.

The rapid application development model, or RAD, was an adaptation of the incremental model for projects that had very restricted time limits, as it was based on the concept of establishing time boxes for the development of each build, in an attempt to bring together IS development and the business goals of the organization (Gottesdiener 1995).

SDLCs can be seen as context-specific applications of the principles of the various system development methodologies. The dichotomy between traditional and agile has a parallel in waterfall versus incremental, albeit not an exact one. While methodologies allow for the organization to position the desired information system within the larger context of the project's needs and goals, development life cycles describe the system's development process in detail, from conception to deployment. Pinpointing the appropriate SDLC for a given project can provide developers with a valuable tool for organization and management.

1.4 IS Development Methodologies

An IS development methodology (ISDM) can be defined as a "system of procedures, techniques, tools, and documentation aids, usually based on some philosophical view, which help the system developers in their efforts to implement a new information system" (Avison and Fitzgerald 1995, cited by Avison and Taylor 1997). Iivari et al. (2001) define IDSM as a set of specific instructions or procedures, constituting a model or general guideline for the goals, tools, and steps necessary to build a system.

Toward the end of the twentieth century, most ISDM that were in practical use by organizations and companies were either *structural* or *object* methodologies (Tumbas and Matkovic 2006). Essentially, structural methodologies were characterized by rigid, step-by-step descriptions of the flow of activities that constitute the development process, from the analysis of the system's requirements to the design and eventual implementation and maintenance of the final product. Each step is rigidly determined, and there are no overlaps. Object methodologies focused on the dynamic aspect of the process of development and perceived each stage in the process as part of an evolutionary chain of events, leading to the notion of iterative or incremental development, where the system is released in a preliminary version, and subsequent versions improve and complete it.

Both structural and object methodologies are now commonly referred to as *traditional methodologies*. In essence, traditional development advocates single-pass development through successive stages, based on extensive documentation and a rigid perception of requirements. Methods outlined under the traditional scope aim at being as simple as possible, because the goal is often to make them adaptable

1.4 IS Development Methodologies

to as many different projects as possible. This led some researchers and developers alike to find such methods inadequate for the fluid nature of development projects (Hardy et al. 1995).

As IT and IS became more complex, developing projects were increasingly constrained by external factors such as budgetary and time limits, unstable user requirements, and the constant evolution of available technology (Tumbas and Matkovic 2006). Toward the end of the 1990s, a new category of ISDM has surfaced that is commonly referred to as agile development, and its increasing popularity has reshaped the research on ISDM during the last decade. The most popular form of agile development in recent years is the scrum methodology (VersionOne 2013), which is particularly flexible and can account for requirement changes at any point of the process, making it ideal for commercial projects (Fig. 1.3).

Avison and Taylor (1997) classify the different ISDM according to five different types, which are ultimately based on the scope of the problem situation that the system aims at resolving. We have summarized these findings in Table 1.1.

The first class consists of well-defined problems, with clear requirements and objectives. This class encompasses the more traditional methodologies, which divide the development process into a given number of stages, starting typically with analysis of requirements and ending with the product's final release and maintenance, with no overlapping between stages (Avison and Taylor 1997). An example is the structured systems analysis and design methodology (SSADM). This methodology follows a set structure of eight stages, starting with strategic planning and feasibility studies, and ending with production, maintenance, and review of the final product (Goodland and Riha 1999). Although later alterations can be made, it is not an incremental methodology, as the product is only released when it is

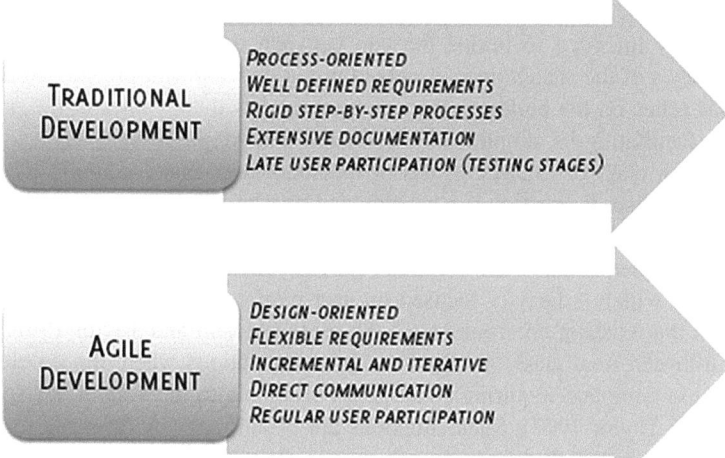

Fig. 1.3 Traditional versus agile development

Table 1.1 Different types of ISDM, based on Avison and Taylor (1997)

Problem situation	Requirements	Methodologies
Well defined	Clear	Technical, rigid, hard approaches. Ex.: SSADM
Well defined	Unstable	Technical, rigid, problem-oriented and focused on tools rather that stages. Ex.: STRADIS
Unstructured	Unstable	Soft approaches, context and user-based. Ex.: SSM
N/A	Unstable	User-centric and focused on subjectivity. Ex.: ETHICS
Complex	Unstable	Contingency models, hybrid approaches. Ex.: Multiview

complete. SSADM was originally intended for use by government entities and large projects, so it is ideal for stable requirements and is heavily reliant on documentation (Schumacher 2001).

The second class of ISDM includes all methodologies that are applicable to well-structured problem situations, where the ultimate goals are clear, but where user requirements are likely to change along the process (Avison and Taylor 1997). Structured analysis and design of information systems (STRADIS) is an example of this class of ISDM. It is essentially a traditional methodology; however, it focuses heavily on the tools necessary to solve specific problems, instead of attempting to outline a generic set of stages that should be followed for all situations, therefore making it a much more problem-oriented solution (Britts 2011).

The third class of ISDM is comprised of methodologies which are applicable to unstructured problem situations, where objectives and requirements are unclear and most likely unstable (Avison and Taylor 1997). Such situations call for an approach that focuses on the wider context of the project, and the subjective views of the users and developers, thus these methodologies are commonly known as "soft" approaches (as opposed to "hard" approaches that emphasize the technical processes and tools). The prime example is the soft systems methodology (SSM) which was precisely intended to bridge the gap between the different (and often conflicting) views of the stakeholders involved in the development project. To achieve this, SSM relies on the building of conceptual models that synthesize the problem situation, facilitating its simplification (Sánchez and Mejía 2008).

The fourth class of ISDM consists of methodologies that are applicable to situations where user interaction is very high and/or where user acceptance is a major factor, such as in highly commercial projects. An example is the effective technical and human implementation and computer-based systems, or ETHICS methodology, an approach which is heavily focused on user participation and the impact of the system on the working environment of the users (Avison and Taylor 1997).

The fifth and final class of ISDM comprises situations where the problem situation is too complex, requiring contingency solutions to the system development (Avison and Taylor 1997). Such situations are usually met by resorting to hybrid methodologies that pick aspects from various others, in order to reach a solution that is appropriate for the particular situation at hand. The Multiview methodology is an example of this hybrid approach.

Essentially, ISD methodologies are specific theoretical constructions of what exactly is necessary to build a system. The great variety of existing methodologies is rooted on the reality that each system has a particular context—not only organizational, but social and technological as well—and the methodology to build that system will be influenced by what particular goals and philosophies the stakeholders are trying to promote or focus on. Thus, methodologies determine the tools and techniques that will be used to create or improve a system and are more specific and practice-oriented constructs of IS research than the previously discussed paradigms.

1.5 Web Site Development Methodologies

Traditionally, projects that involved the creation and development of Web applications and sites were managed much in the same way as any other software development projects, and the corresponding methodologies were used. However, even during the first years of widespread commercial use of the internet, researchers have pointed out that there are very particular aspects to Web development which give rise to particular needs, when it comes to developing a new product or system.

Developers had been faced with this reality, but the solution was often to implement ad hoc strategies, without the systematic, methodical, and rigorous approach that characterized traditional software development. This issue was further emphasized by the rapid growth of the Internet and the perceived need by many companies and organizations to quickly "be on the Web," leading to rushed development processes (Murugesan et al. 2001).

In 1998, a group of researchers and developers attempted to address this issue in the first Workshop on Web Engineering, where Web Engineering was presented as a new discipline of software engineering, focusing on the inherent aspects of Web development that require appropriate solutions. A set of guidelines was determined, essentially adapting key constructs from software development methodologies to the reality of the Web. Their ultimate goal was to establish "sound scientific, engineering and management principles and disciplined and systematic approaches to the successful development, deployment and maintenance of high quality web-based systems and applications" (Murugesan et al. 2001).

In Web development, there is more emphasis on design as a process stage, because Web developers cannot control the environment in which potential users are going to use the product. A wide variety of user preferences, as well as the awareness of existing competition, create a prominent need to make the Web site or application immediately distinctive and usable, thus making design a fundamental aspect, and introducing a component of esthetic creativity that is not present in traditional software development.

The object-oriented hypermedia design methodology (OOHDM), proposed in 1995 by Schwabe and Rossi, breaks down the design process into three dimensions: conceptual design, navigational design, and abstract interface design, after which follows the stage of implementation of the product. Conceptual design involves the creation of a conceptual model of the Web site that produces a set of classes, subsystems, and their relationships. Navigational design implies the description and visualizations of the navigational structure of the Web site, through varied navigational classes such as nodes, links, indexes, and tours. The abstract interface design then interprets the conceptual model and the navigational structure into interface classes—text fields, buttons, etc. Throughout the entire design process, OOHDM uses object-oriented modeling as its main tool, hence its name (Schwabe et al. 1999). It is ultimately a methodology that aims at helping developers and designers create single-user hypermedia environments, but researchers have observed that it is not adequate to projects that want to embed authoring functions in the Web site or application, permitting users to edit and add content (Schümmer et al. 1999).

Similarly, the relationship management methodology (RMM) focused on hypermedia applications, as the vehicle for the relationships between objects. Developed by Isakowitz et al. (1995), it is a structured, step-by-step methodology. The process starts with rigorous analysis of the Web site's objectives, the market, and the user base, as well as information sources, permissions, distribution channels, and other business-related principles. Then, much like the OODHM, the design process is broken apart, in this case, in six stages related to different dimensions of design, as outlined in Fig. 1.4.

While OOHDM and RMM are adaptations of traditional, rigid IS development methodologies, other methodologies have attempted to bring a more holistic approach to Web development, in accordance with the large scope of goals and needs of Web projects. The Web information system development methodology (WISDM) was developed by Vidgen et al. (2002) in an attempt to combine essential principles of the Multiview IS development methodology with the specific characteristics of Web projects. Multiview is a contingent, goal-oriented solution to the development of IS projects with complex and diffuse needs and requirements. Likewise, WISDM posits that a unified approach that brings together the different levels of the development project, proposing a socio-technical approach. The development process is broken apart into a four-stage framework. The analysis stage is divided into organizational analysis (where goals of the Web project are integrated into the organization's general strategy) and information analysis (where

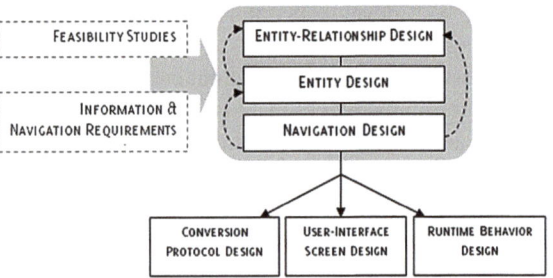

Fig. 1.4 Design processes of the RMM (adapted from Isakowitz et al. 1995)

requirements are specified). The design stage is also divided into two processes: work design (where the characteristics of the Web project are developed in line with user/customer needs) and technical design (where the project is physically developed through programming), while user-interface design bridges the two processes. This methodology stands out due to its heavy emphasis on the creative aspects of Web development, while more traditional methodologies are too reliant on IS-specific terminology and principles.

Much like IS development methodologies, all Web development methodologies ultimately aim at aiding in the creation of products that are efficient and appropriate not just to the organization's goals, but to the users. However, Web methodologies forcibly need to take new aspects into account, namely an exceedingly diffuse user base which cannot be contacted directly for the most part, and the need to differentiate the product at an esthetic level, so as to permit users having a first contact with the Web site or application to immediately feel a positive relationship with the content. This has introduced specific characteristics to the Web development methodologies, namely a great emphasis on design processes.

1.6 Usability Evaluation Models

In IS development research, one question in particular has generated a considerable amount of attention: How can developers and managers effectively determine whether given IS are being successful in accomplishing the goals they were developed for? How to assess the degree to which the system is improving the general working principles of its users?

The issue of usability is of key importance in this field. Usability essentially refers to the degree to which a system is easily learned and used by its users. Some researchers have focused on the study of cognitive processes as a way to define usability principles that are directly inferred from those processes, hence more appropriately matched to the way users behave and think.

According to Norman (1993), there are two dimensions to human cognitive processes. The experiential mode refers to perceptions, actions, and reactions, while the reflective mode implies thinking, reasoning, comparing, and making logical decisions. It is argued that specific modes of cognitive experience require different technologies and systems. The proposed field of cognitive engineering specifically focuses on the development of systems that support users' cognitive processes, in an attempt to facilitate the adjustment to the system, and reduce the difficulty and complexity of the system, using human–computer interaction (HCI) principles.

Similarly, to this approach, researchers have attempted to define models so as to aid developers in determining the adequacy of their system to their respective users, during the testing and evaluation stages of the development process. Nielsen (1994) observed a number of different methods of evaluating usability, summarized as follows:

- Heuristic evaluation—informal methods where usability experts evaluate HCI dialogues according to established principles (heuristics), specific to the project;
- Cognitive walkthroughs—detailed procedures where a user's problem solving process is simulated, and it is analyzed whether the process will lead to the correct, expected actions or not;
- Formal usability inspections—rigid procedures that follow well-defined roles and combine heuristic evaluations with simplified forms of cognitive walkthroughs;
- Pluralistic walkthroughs—meetings where users, developers, and other stakeholders discuss scenarios and dialogue elements;
- Feature inspection—a thorough inspection of features, sequences, processes, and all aspects that users can eventually come across, pinpointing what aspects are exceedingly unnatural or require excessive experience/knowledge;
- Consistency inspection—the designers inspect and compare interface features from multiple projects;
- Standards inspection—an expert on a specific interface standard inspects the project for compliance.

There have been other methods and methodologies established for the better evaluation of usability. Card et al. (1983) proposed the GOMS model, where four essential constructs are emphasized—goals, operators, methods, and selection rules, giving the model its acronym. Goals are the specification of user needs and objectives. Operators are the specific objects that will physically describe the HCI. Methods are programs built from the operators, designed to facilitate the accomplishment of the goals. Selection rules then help predicting which method will be more appropriate for specific situations. The ultimate goal of this methodology is to bridge the gap between the psychological level, where the users' cognitive processes develop, and the concrete, physical level, where the system acts.

Pirolli and Card (1999) in turn describe an adaptive control of thought in information foraging model (ACT-IF) which is essentially derived from the theories of evolutionary psychology. The process by which users search and gather information is illustratively compared to the process of food foraging, and it is asserted that users will follow "scents," which, in the context of IS, are the perceptions of value, cost, accessibility, obtained from instinctive cues such as citations, links, and icons. The stronger and more evident these cues are, the more likely the user is to make correct choices that fulfill his/her needs. Thus, developers need to focus on methods to appropriately direct users to the information they need.

Usability evaluation models are always interrelated with psychological concepts, particularly in the field of cognitive theory, and research in one field accompanies research on the other field. Resorting to essential principles and theories on how the human mind seeks and absorbs new information and new knowledge, researchers on IS usability have attempted to use those principles to establish good practices of development, where developers of new systems take into account the basics of human psychology to build systems that adequately adjust to the psychological framework of its users. This is a means to ensure that the system is successfully accepted.

1.7 Quality Evaluation Models

Technology acceptance has been a very active subject of research, not just for the field of IS, but for marketing as well. For developers and managers alike, it is crucial to evaluate by which processes will users or customers adopt and successfully accept a given system or technology, or reject it altogether. In order to determine this, the stage of implementation, as well as any other stages following that, is fundamental. It is also of key importance to understand the constitution of the user base, its contextual background, their needs, objectives, and obstacles. Finally, researchers have also borrowed concepts from behavioral psychology, going to the deeper level of human behavior to understand the processes by which people make their choices to use or discard tools.

A pioneering approach on this issue was the theory of reasoned action (TRA), developed by Fishbein and Ajzen (1975). It asserts that there are four different variables that influence behavioral action: beliefs, attitudes, intentions, and behaviors. The model describes the relationships between these factors. Essentially, beliefs and evaluations shape the user's attitude toward behavior; normative beliefs and the user's motivation to comply with them shape the subjective norm. Beliefs and subjective norm will then shape the user's behavioral intention, leading to a result of an actual behavior. This premise was later adjusted by Ajzen (1991) in his theory of planned behavior (TPB), where the relationships and variables involved in the process are analyzed in more depth. According to the TPB model, beside behavioral and normative beliefs, there is a third factor that will influence the user's intentions: control beliefs, related to the user's perception of whether he/she can effectively use the new system. Both TRA and TPB models are essentially behavioral theory models that can be adapted to the context of IS acceptance.

However, one of the most popular approaches on this field was the technology acceptance model (TAM), proposed by Davis (1986). It describes the means by which subjective elements, such as a user's perception of the system's usefulness, will influence objective elements, such as system use. Once key design features are implemented and also considering other external influences (such as personal context, organizational structure, and socioeconomic background), users will form a cognitive response based on their perception of the new system's functionality and usability (perceived usefulness). This will generate an affective response, translated in their attitude toward use of the system, and eventually a behavioral response, which is the actual use of the system (or its rejection). This model thus establishes a causal relationship between user's perceptions of the system and their choice to use it (see Fig. 1.5).

TAM is an exceedingly simple model, which has led it to be a very popular option for researchers, because it can easily be adjusted to a variety of contexts. On the other hand, it has also been the subject of frequent criticism, namely due to the vague characterization of its core constructs and relationships. For this reason, there have been attempts at building more consistent and complex models on this simple premise. Venkatesh and Davis (2000) proposed the TAM 2, whose ultimate goal

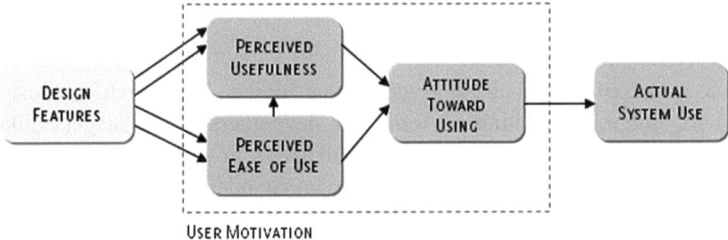

Fig. 1.5 Technology acceptance model (adapted from Davis 1986)

was to provide a description of the specific mechanisms by which perceived usefulness is formed, considering that it was the most fundamental factor in the original TAM model.

Essentially, all quality evaluation models have attempted to bring together the key aspects that form or influence user's cognitive processes and behavioral decisions. Venkatesh et al. (2003) combined eight existing models found in previous literature to create what they described as the unified theory of acceptance and use of technology (UTAUT). They started by outlining a list of constructs used in the existing models and pinpointed which constructs appeared to more useful and significant in empirical research. From there, they determined that the more important factors of user acceptance could be summarized in four variables: performance expectancy, effort expectancy, social influence, and facilitating conditions. External factors, such as gender, age, experience, and voluntariness of use, acted as moderating elements over those variables. The differing levels of impact resulted in particular behavioral intentions, and use behaviors.

These and other models of technology and IS acceptance have in common the importance of individual perceptions, although different theories consider different factors to be of influence in shaping those perceptions. These models are particularly useful for developers and designers, allowing them to adjust the models to the project, and determine what factors will most likely determine the user's acceptance of the final released product.

1.8 IS Models for Success Assessment

As we have seen, the concept of IS success has been closely interrelated with the concept of user acceptance, in accordance with behavioral theories. The pioneering work of DeLone and McLean (1992) established the basics for the creation of a model of IS success assessment, centered on the premise that use of the system is intimately related with user satisfaction. It attempted to describe the acceptance of a system through a causal–explanatory approach, where use and user satisfaction, constantly feeding on each other, directly influence individual impact, which eventually reflects on organizational impact (Iivari 2002). This model was later

1.8 IS Models for Success Assessment

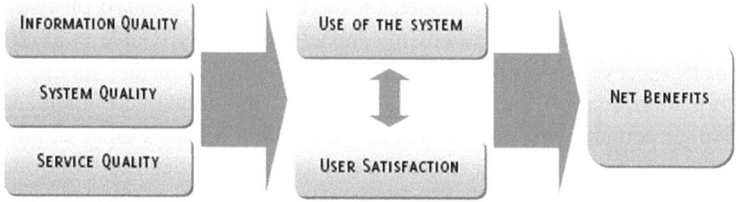

Fig. 1.6 D&M model of IS success (adapted from DeLone and McLean 2003)

adapted by the authors to include a more comprehensive perspective of system quality and a more encompassing concept of organizational impact (described as net benefits of the system) (see Fig. 1.6).

The authors argued that for a model of IS success to be truly useful, it had to have as few variables as possible, so as to make it suitable for the great variety of different realities and systems that exist in practice (DeLone and McLean 2003), and this principle justifies the model's simplicity, which has made it one of the most popular—and scrutinized—approaches to IS success in research.

Seddon (1997) attempted to break down the simple concepts of the D&M model by offering a slightly different perspective, particularly on the idea of use/user satisfaction. The subsequent model, named the Seddon model, substituted the concept of use by that of perceived usefulness, thus introducing expectations as key variables in the process. Expectations about the net benefits of future use of the system will lead to use of the system (Seddon 1997). Use, in itself, is not a measure of success but a behavior. User satisfaction, on the other hand, is influenced by a great number of factors, including system quality, information quality, perceived usefulness, individual net benefits, organizational net benefits, and societal net benefits. Later adjustments of the Seddon model introduced the concepts of group impact and external impact, to account for the influences that the user can be subjected to from his/her peers or from his/her social context (Kurian et al. 2000).

Other authors have equally attempted to build on the D&M model, expanding or breaking apart some of its essential concepts, particularly user satisfaction.

The 3D model (Ballantine et al. 1996) analyzed the concept of IS success as a three-dimensional construct related to three different stages of IS development: development, deployment, and delivery. Development pertains to the actual creation of the system (design, coding, etc.). For the system to be successfully deployed, it has to cross a barrier called the implementation filter, comprised mainly of factors relating to the user's expectations, involvement, experience, and possibility of choice. After the system's been deployed—used by its users—there is an integration filter, where factors such as strategy, organizational culture, and organizational structure will determine the degree to which the system fits in with the existing organization. Finally, for the system to be successfully delivered, it has to pass the environmental filter, where competitor movements and economic and political contexts exert their influence (Ballantine et al. 1996).

The IS impact measurement model, on the other hand, focused on two fundamental aspects of success measurement: impact and quality (Gable et al. 2008). It describes IS success as a result of a combination of different factors: quality (system and information quality), satisfaction, and impact (individual and organizational). Instead of perceiving these factors as elements within a causal process, all factors are independent and exert their influence through various degrees, with one common output, IS success. Notably, this model does not consider use of the system as a significant factor, because there are various instances where system use does not depend on other variables and is mandatory regardless of user perceptions, leading the authors to exclude it (Gable et al. 2008).

The success of a given information system within its organization is a difficult aspect to describe with precision, because it is subjected to numerous influences. Different researchers are focused on different variables with more or less emphasis, leading to the creation of various models whose adequacy to describe IS success will depend on the purpose of this assessment. Simpler models such as D&M are ideal for broader considerations. But more specific, quantitative approaches will require more complex models, such as the 3D model.

1.9 Conclusions

We have analyzed the key aspects and contributions to the body of research on IS development and success measurement. Paradigms, methodologies, SDLC models, and success evaluation models are all theoretical constructs that aim at systemically describing the complex reality of IS, in a way that simplifies not just future research, but also the work of developers and managers in determining the principles and methods of their projects.

There are three degrees for the theoretical approach to IS, illustrated in Fig. 1.7. Paradigms offer the broadest perspective, ultimately consisting on the insertion of different approaches to IS development within the context of a particular philosophy or global view on goals and requirements.

At the development level, IS development methodologies, systems development life cycles, and Web development methodologies propose varied systematic approaches to the development process, describing sets of stages, activities, and roles necessary to achieve successful and efficient development.

Finally, usability models, quality evaluation models, and success assessment models allow managers and developers to determine the degree to which the system is adequate to the goals, needs, and intentions of the users.

As we have seen, the characteristics of the project determine what model or methodology should be adopted in order to facilitate the development process. In that sense, a comprehensive study of the different approaches and methods of IS development can be a valuable tool for developers. We have determined that there are two principles of IS development: traditional, structured, rigid methods and agile, incremental, flexible methods. The first category is suitable for large projects,

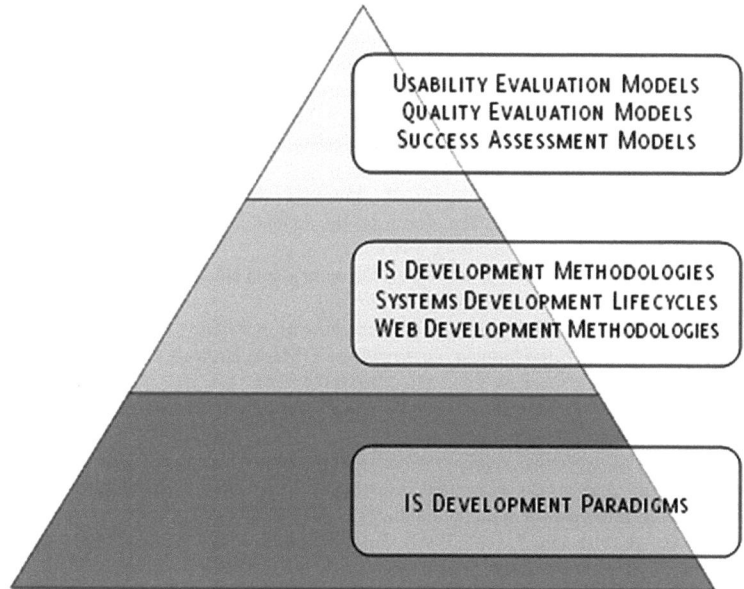

Fig. 1.7 Different levels of IS research

where requirements are well established, face-to-face communication is not efficient (as opposed to documentation), and user participation is not necessary at all times. A good example is government projects, where methodical organization and rigor are essential. The second category is suitable for medium- to small-sized projects, heavily user-centered, where requirements are likely to change and there is constant feedback between developers and users alike. This is the ideal approach for many commercial software projects.

In regard to evaluation of the project, usability models are appropriate primarily to determine how the system can closely interrelate with the user's cognitive and learning processes, thus facilitating their adaptation to it. Quality evaluation models allow developers to determine what will shape the user's acceptance of the new system, and success evaluation models will help developers in measuring the implementation of the system, providing valuable metrics and feedback for future updates and/or systems.

References

Ajzen, I. (1991). The theory of planned behavior. *Organizational Behavior and Human Decision Processes, 50*(2), 179–211.

Alter, S. (2008). Defining Information Systems as work systems: Implications for the IS field. *Business Analytics and Information Systems,* Paper 22.

Avison, D. E., & Fitzgerald, G. (1995). *Information systems development: Methodologies, techniques and tools*, 2nd edn. London: McGraw-Hill.

Avison, D. E., & Taylor, V. (1997). Information Systems development methodologies: A classification according to problem situation. *Journal of Information Technology, 12*, 73–81.

Balaji, S., & Murugaiyan, M. (2012). Waterfall vs. V-Model vs. Agile: A comparative study on SDLC. *International Journal of Information Technology and Business Management, 2*(1), 26–30.

Ballantine, J., Bonner, M., Levy, M., Martin, A., Munro, I., & Powell, P. (1996). The 3-D model of Information Systems success: The search for the dependent variable continues. *Information Resources Management Journal, 9*(4), 5–15.

Boehm, B. (1988). A Spiral model of software development and enhancement. *IEEE Computer, 21*(5), 61–72.

Britts, W. (2011). *The relationship between organizational and national culture and the use and effectiveness of systems development methodologies* (Master's thesis, North-West University). Retrieved from http://dspace.nwu.ac.za/handle/10394/9165

Card, S., Moran, T. P., & Newell, A. (1983). *The Psychology of human computer interaction*. Hillsdale: Lawrence Erlbaum Associates.

Davis, F. (1986). *A technology acceptance model for empirically testing new end-user Information Systems: Theory and results*. (Doctoral dissertation, Massachusetts Institute of Technology). Retrieved from http://dspace.mit.edu/handle/1721.1/15192

DeLone, W. H., & McLean, E. R. (1992). Information Systems success: The quest for the dependent variable. *Information Systems Research, 3*(1), 60–95.

DeLone, W. H., & McLean, E. R. (2003). The DeLone and McLean model of Information Systems success: A ten-year update. *Journal of Management Information Systems, Spring 2003, 19*(4), 9–30.

Fishbein, M., & Ajzen, I. (1975). *Belief, attitude, intention and behavior: An introduction to theory and research*. Reading: Addison-Wesley.

Gable, G., Sedera, D., & Chan, T. (2008). Re-conceptualizing Information Systems success: The IS-impact measurement model. *Journal of the Association for Information Systems, 9*(7), 377–408.

Goodland, M., & Riha, K. (1999). SSADM—An introduction. Retrieved from http://www.dcs.bbk.ac.uk/~steve/1/index.htm

Gottesdiener, E. (1995). RAD realities: Beyond the hype to how RAD really works. *Application Development Trends, August 1995*, 29–38.

Hardy, C., Thompson, J., & Edwards, H. (1995). The use, limitation and customization of structured systems development methods in the United Kingdom. *Information and Software Technology, 37*(9), 467–477.

Hirschheim, R., & Klein, H. (1989). Four paradigms of information systems development. *Communications of the ACM, 32*(10), 1199–1216.

Iivari, J. (2002). An empirical test of the DeLone-McLean model of Information System success. *The Data Base for Advances in Information Systems, 36*(2), 8–27.

Iivari, J., & Hirschheim, R. (1996). Analyzing Information Systems development: A comparison and analysis of eight IS development approaches. *Information Systems, 21*(7), 551–575.

Iivari, J., Hirschheim, R., & Klein, H. (1998). A paradigmatic analysis contrasting Information Systems development approaches and methodologies. *Information Systems Research, 9*(2), 164–193.

Iivari, J., Hirschheim, R., & Klein, H. (2001). A dynamic framework for classifying Information Systems development methodologies and approaches. *Journal of Management Information Systems, 17*(3), 179–218.

Isakowitz, T., Stohr, E. A., & Balasubramaninan, P. (1995). RMM: A methodology for structured Hypermedia design. *Communications of the ACM, 38*(8), 34–44.

Kurian, D., Gallupe, R., & Diaz, J. (2000). Taking stock: Measuring Information Systems success. *ASAC-IFSAM-2000 Proceedings, 21*, 77–90.

References

Massey, V., & Satao, K. (2012). Comparing various SDLC models and the new proposed model on the basis of available methodology. *International Journal of Advanced Research in Computer Science and Software Engineering, 2*(4), 170–177.

Munassar, N., & Govardhan, A. (2010). Comparison between five models of software engineering. *International Journal of Computer Science Issues, 7*(5), 94–101.

Murugesan, S., Deshpande, Y., Hansen, S., & Ginige, A. (2001). Web engineering: A new discipline for development of Web-based systems. In S. Murugesan & Y. Deshpande (Eds.), *Web engineering: Managing diversity and complexity of Web application development* (pp. 3–13). Berlin, Heildelberg: Springer.

Nielsen, J. (1994). Usability inspection methods. *Conference Companion on Human Factors in Computing Systems* (pp. 413–414). New York: ACM.

Norman, D. (1993). *Things that make us smart.* : Addison-Wesley.

Nunamaker, J., Chen, M., & Purdin, T. (1991). Systems development in Information Systems research. *Journal of Management Information Systems, 7*(3), 89–106.

Patterson Jr., F. (2004). Life cycles for system acquisition. In Encyclopedia of Life Support Systems, *Systems Engineering and Management for Sustainable Development* (pp. 82–110). Retrieved from http://www.eolss.net/ebooks/Sample%20Chapters/C15/E1-28-01-02.pdf

Pirolli, P., & Card, S. (1999). Information foraging. *Psychological Review, 106*, 643–675.

Royce, W. (1970). Managing the development of large software systems. In *Proceedings of the IEEE WESCON, August 1970* (pp. 1–9).

Sánchez, A., & Mejía, A. (2008). Learning to support learning together: An experience with the Soft systems methodology. *Educational Action Research, 16*(1), 109–124.

Schumacher, M. (2001). *The use of SSADM (Structured Systems Analysis and Design Methodology) as a standard methodology on information systems projects.* Retrieved from http://www.grin.com/en/e-book/106034/the-use-of-ssadm-structured-systems-analysis-and-design-methodology-as

Schümmer, J., Schuckmann, C., Bibbó, L., & Zapico, J. (1999). Collaborative Hypermedia design patterns in OOHDM. In *Proceedings of the HT99 Workshop on Hypermedia Development — Design Patterns in Hypermedia, Darmstadt.*

Schwabe, D., Pontes, R. A., & Moura, I. (1999). OOHDM-Web: An environment for implementation of Hypermedia applications in the WWW. *ACM SigWEB Newsletter, 8*(2).

Seddon, P. B. (1997). A respecification and extension of the DeLone and McLean Model of IS success. *Information Systems Research, 8*(3), 240–253.

Tumbas, P., & Matkovic, P. (2006). Agile vs. Traditional methodologies in developing Information Systems. *Management Information Systems, 1*(2006), 15–24.

Venkatesh, V., & Davis, F. D. (2000). A theoretical extension of the technology acceptance model: Four longitudinal field studies. *Management Science, 46*(2), 186–204.

Venkatesh, V., Morris, M., Davis, G., & Davis, F. (2003). User acceptance of information technology: Toward a unified view. *MIS Quarterly, 27*, 425–478.

VersionOne (2013). *8th Annual State of Agile development survey.* Retrieved from http://stateofagile.versionone.com/

Vidgen, R., Avison, D., Wood, B., & Wood-Harper, T. (2002). *Developing web information systems.* Oxford: Butterworth-Heinemann.

Zachman, J. A. (1987). A framework for Information Systems architecture. *IBM Systems Journal, 26*(3), 276–292.

Chapter 2
Information System Development Life Cycle Models

2.1 Introduction

With the increasing evolution and complexity of information technologies, there has emerged a multiplicity of applications for information systems (IS): They assist in corporate transactions, they connect business and office data, and they support users in the architecture of strategy. The complexity of their nature and objectives requires the harnessing of technology and user experience to create systems that meet their expected purpose. In essence, system development consists of this process of creating an information system, with all the variables that it entails and which usually need to be taken into account: its ability to be user-friendly, how well it functions, if it meets the needs of the organization in which it will be integrated, and so forth.

The life cycle of an IS development begins with its creation and ends with its termination. Along this process, it goes through various stages, which have been discussed to some extension in existing literature. Cohen (2010) outlines "requirements, analysis, design, construction (or coding), testing (validation), installation, operation, maintenance, and the less emphasized retirement" as the key components of the development process. According to Jirava (2004), the conventional "life cycle is composed of five phases: Investigation, User Requirements, Analysis, Design, Implementation and Release."

Generally speaking, the life cycle is perceived as the time frame that spans from the development of a new system to its eventual retirement. It is a process that starts with the emergence of an idea, goes through its implementation, and ends with its termination, moving across all the intermediate stages in which its viability and usability are prioritized (Jirava 2004).

However, IS are very complex structures. They are built with a specific goal, for a specific organization. Because of this specificity, each system development process requires a guiding framework to configure, outline, and monitor the progress of the development along all the stages of the life cycle. Although the methods employed in this framework depend on the peculiar characteristics of each project, it is possible to ascertain that there are key components that all congruent frameworks must necessarily entail. The most notable one is the segmentation of the development process into phases, with each phase having a beginning, an end, a series of specific activities, deliverables (documentation that is prepared regularly to ensure performance accountability for each required task), and monitoring tools. Cohen (2010) notes that this same principle is also true for the introduction of IS not through their development in house, but through external acquisition (the purchase of a set of software applications from an external vendor). Both imply a process of implementation, maturing, and termination.

The core objective of the development or implementation of a system is its efficient integration in real-life situations. Therefore, two of the primordial steps in the life cycle are the assessment of what the different people involved in the system's use will require and a knowledge of the context in which the system will be operated. The negligence of these two essential elements is at the origin of several issues in systems' use in real settings (Tetlay and John 2009). The usability aspect of a system is central, that is why the inclusion of the user in the entirety of the development life cycle is crucial. For developers, it is paramount to have all the correct information regarding the users' needs. Misinformation has repercussions on the development of the system, and it usually results in the implementation of products that fall short of the users' expectations and have a diminished productivity. It is important to potentiate the users' participation, namely by informing them about how the development process works and the need for accurate information (Durrani and Qureshi 2012).

However, even considering these crucial common points that all frameworks must necessarily include, the methodology for system development has a great variety of approaches, which we call models of system development life cycle (SDLC). Some of the most commonly cited are the spiral, waterfall, V-shaped, and agile models. Given the multiplicity of research studies on this field, it is crucial to outline an overview of them, to help further understand which one of them would be more appropriate for a specific project. The point where the model or framework that will guide the development process is chosen is a central strategic aspect that will undeniably have an impact on the effectiveness of the system in the long run. The wrong life cycle can delay the project and affect client satisfaction, and it can even mean the cancelation of the system (Executive Brief 2008).

In this paper, we will offer a panoramic overview of the most significant models of SDLC, which will present a useful tool for the embryonic stages of any IS development process.

2.2 The Waterfall Model

The waterfall model was introduced by Royce in (1970), specifically in the context of spacecraft mission software design, and is one of the most popular methods of assessing the evolution of a product or system. Essentially, it is a step-by-step sequential description of the product's life cycle that spans 7 different stages, originally denominated "system requirements, software requirements, analysis, program design, coding, testing and operations" (Royce 1970).

The first premise in which this model is based is that any development process of any software or system starts off by two essential steps: analysis and coding. This is the simplest conceptualization of the model, but is ineffective to understand the product's further development beyond the stage of creation. Therefore, the analysis stage is broken down into two steps—analysis of both system and software requirements, while the coding stage is preceded by program design (Royce 1970).

The essence of the waterfall model is that it attempts to provide a useful set of guidelines for the development of new programs or systems. In his original work, Royce (1970) provides five key principles that he believes are essential for the successful development of large software systems.

The first is "program design comes first." It is essential to allow designers to be a part of the initial process, because of their invaluable feedback regarding resources and limitations. The second is "document the design." Extensive documentation of the development process is paramount, not just to facilitate management of the process, but to facilitate performance assessments, making the eventual correction of mistakes more efficient. The third is "do it twice," referring that the final version of the product should actually be the second version, where all the stages have been performed and it is easier to pinpoint strengths and weaknesses, to emphasize the first and correct the latter. The fourth is "plan, control and monitor testing." Testing is a fundamental stage. It is important to bring in specialists that did not participate in the earlier stages of the process. It is also important to test every single aspect of the project, regardless of how relevant it is. Finally, the fifth guideline is "involve the customer." Having the insight, judgment, and commitment of the customer taken into account during the development process is a viable option that will greatly improve its potential for general acceptance (Royce 1970).

The waterfall model was a popular approach, and for that reason, it evolved and adapted into numerous forms, according to different research studies and the context of application. Denomination of each step varies greatly and can reflect the specific objective of the study or the field in which it is applied.

However, one common trait covers all the variations of this model: it is a sequential model. Each of its stages must be entirely concluded before the next can begin. Similarly to the flow of a waterfall, the development of the software is regarded as continuously streaming downward throughout its different stages (Massey and Satao 2012). Thus, for example, analysis of requirements must be thorough and final before design begins, and testing can only be efficiently carried out once coding is entirely complete. Each stage is regarded as a static component, a rigid step in the process. Subsequent changes in previous steps (e.g., awareness of new requirements) cannot be taken into account (Balaji and Murugaiyan 2012) (Fig. 2.1).

The waterfall model took precedence over other models in the 1980s and the beginning of the 1990s. But this preponderance suffered an important setback with the increasing speed of technological evolution and the subsequent need to swiftly

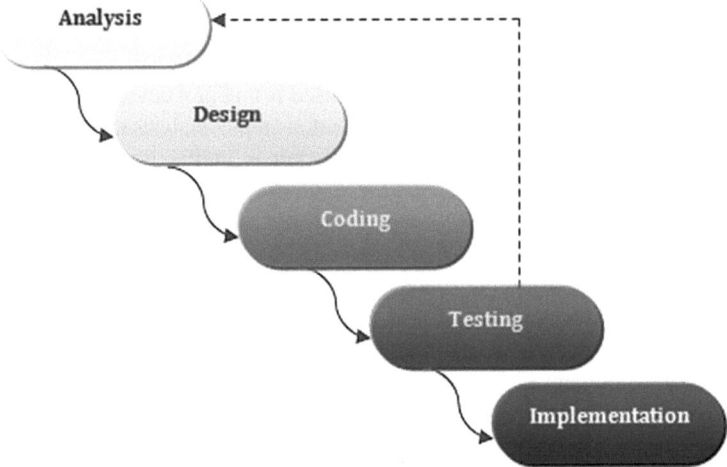

Fig. 2.1 An example of the waterfall life cycle model (adapted from Balaji and Murugaiyan 2012)

deliver new software systems and products. Viewing each stage as a single, "frozen" moment of evolution can greatly delay the implementation stage because errors will only be detected very late in the process, during the testing phase, which is preceded by extensive designing and coding (Munassar and Govardhan 2010). The communication of objectives between developers and clients is also greatly hindered because if the client changes the requirements of the system, the development process needs to completely restart for those changes to be taken into account (Balaji and Murugaiyan 2012).

This model is an idealized and greatly simplified concept of SDLC. It is not very flexible, but it is still popular as a conceptual basis for other frameworks or models. Its greatest strength lies in that it outlines generally accepted positive habits of software development, such as minute and accurate planning early in the project, extensive documentation of the entire process, and having robust design concepts before starting to code (Munassar and Govardhan 2010). However, the reality of a development process can often be much more disorganized than that.

2.3 The Incremental Model

The incremental model is a particular evolution of the waterfall model that attempts to address its more prominent shortcoming, which is the slowness of the cycle. It also aims at outlining a more flexible process that requires less extensive planning up-front (Munassar and Govardhan 2010).

According to this approach, instead of dividing the SDLC into static, isolated steps, the whole process can instead be designed, tested, and implemented one

2.3 The Incremental Model

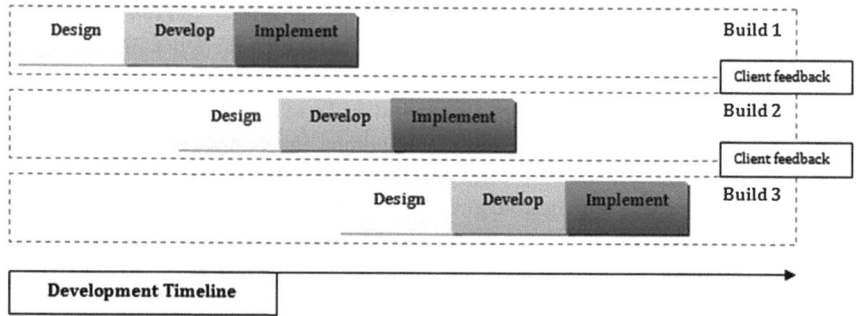

Fig. 2.2 An example of the incremental life cycle model (adapted from Tilloo 2013)

fraction at a time, in successive stages, so that with each stage (or increment), there can be at least some feedback from the client. This feedback will provide valuable assistance in the next increment of the process and so forth. With each ongoing increment, the product is extensively tested and improved, according to objectives and expectations from the client, which facilitates its eventual success (Massey and Satao 2012) (Fig. 2.2).

With this SDLC model, the process of software development is made by increments, through a series of different releases. When the product is launched, when it has its first increment, it is ready for consumer use. Then, according to the clients' response to the software, new increments are made to improve the product. The increments will continue to be added, until the completion of the final product (Massey and Satao 2012).

Each stage is scheduled and structured to allow the development of parts of the system at varied rates and times and to incorporate them into the global project when they are finished. Thus, this model highlights the sequential process of the different phases of development while also trying to maximize the benefits of allowing changes, improvements, and additions to be made between each increment. Development is broken into smaller efforts. These are consistently monitored, so that progress can be accompanied and measured (Texas Project Delivery Framework 2008).

This model fundamentally outlines a progressive development process through the gradual addition of more features, until the completion of the system. It is a more flexible method, because it allows for the incorporation of needs that might not have been obvious at the start of the process, and it facilitates the changes that come with later assessment of different requirements. Additionally, since it builds on each of the phases, it allows for wider amplitude of improvement in the following stages (Executive Brief 2008). Thus, product delivery is not only faster, but it is also easier to test and eventually correct.

However, the downside to this approach is that it can be more costly to develop and release multiple versions of the product. On the other hand, when a later increment is developed due to a new found problem or necessity, it can have compatibility issues with earlier versions of the product (Tilloo 2013).

There is a variation of the incremental model, named the iterative and incremental development model (IIDM). While very similar to incremental, this model puts greater emphasis on the relationships that occur with each increment and between them. These relationships, or iterations, form a cycle or pattern of feedbacks and outputs. In that regard, while maintaining the essence of the incremental model, the IIDM is a more fluid description of development. At the same time, it also allows more space and significance for feedback, as it modifies the scheduling strategy to include specific time frames for revision and improvement of each increment, so that successful conclusion of the development process is more likely at the first final version (Cockburn 2008).

2.4 The Spiral Life Cycle Model

The spiral model dates back to the end of the 1980s, when it was outlined by Barry Boehm, and introduces something that other models did not take into account, which is risk analysis. In essence, the spiral model attempts to bring together key aspects of some other prominent models (namely the waterfall, incremental, and evolutionary prototyping), in an attempt to gather the most appropriate traits from each one, because specific projects might be more or less adaptable to specific models.

According to this SDLC model, the process of developing a system consists of a series of cycles or iterations. Each cycle begins with the identification of objectives and requirements of the current stage, as well as an analysis of alternatives and constraints. This process will highlight areas of uncertainty (risk), which will be taken into account during the next step, the outlining of a strategy or plan, through prototyping and other simulation methods. This process involves constant improvement of the prototype as risks are decreased (while others may arise). Once the prototype becomes sufficiently robust, and risk is reduced to acceptable levels, the next step develops in accordance with the basic waterfall approach, through a succession of stages: concept, requirements, design, and implementation (Boehm 1988). Once this cycle is concluded, another cycle begins, as a new increment of the product is created.

The spiral model bears some resemblance to the incremental life cycle, but the emphasis on risk evaluation presents a major difference. The stages or spirals that constitute this model regard planning as a first step, moving then to the exploration of what the requirements are and subsequently calculating the risks. In this stage of risk calculation, the model is structured to initiate a process of determination of risks and of formulation of alternatives (Massey and Satao 2012); thus, risk management can be considered the centerpiece of the model (Fig. 2.3).

Boehm (2000) asserts that each cycle or iteration of the process will invariably display six particular characteristics, which he named the "invariants."

2.4 The Spiral Life Cycle Model

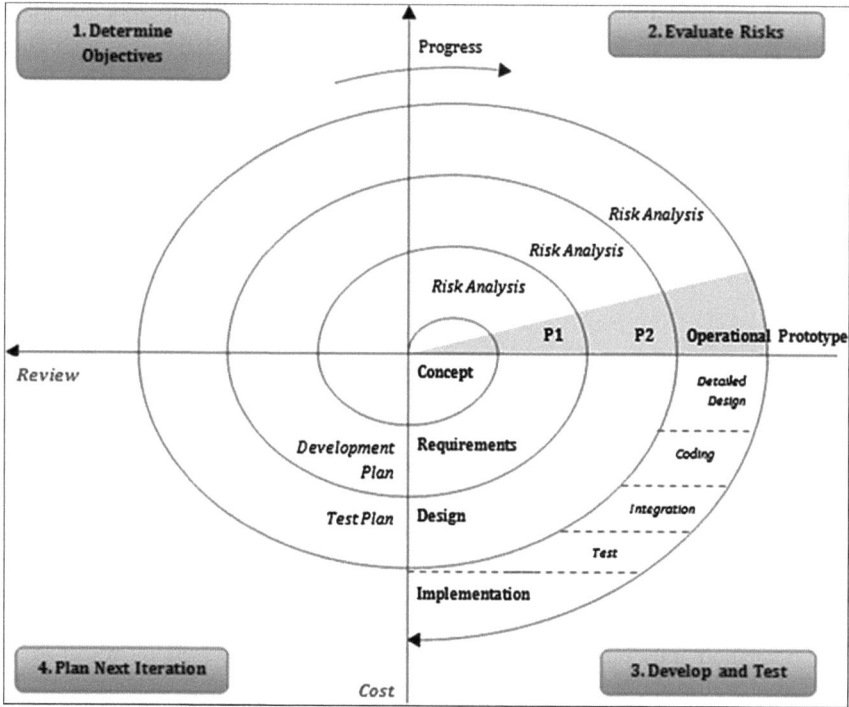

Fig. 2.3 A summary of the spiral development model (adapted from Boehm 1988)

Invariant 1 is the *concurrent definition of key artifacts*, such as concept, requirements, plan, design, and coding. It is argued that defining these artifacts in a sequential structure can constraint the project to excessively rigid preconceptions.

Invariant 2 is that *each cycle follows the four strategic principles that correspond to the four quadrants of the model*: determine objectives, evaluate risks, develop and test, and plan the next iteration. Not moving in accordance with this basic strategy can negatively affect the entire process.

Invariant 3 is that *the level of effort is determined by the risk considerations*. Reasonable time frames must be established for each project in accordance with risk assessments, to determine "how much is enough" in each activity.

Invariant 4 is that *the degree of detail is driven by risk considerations*. Just like invariant 3, here it is important to determine "how much detail is enough" in each stage of the process.

Invariant 5 refers to *the use of anchor point milestones*, which Boehm describes as "Life Cycle Objectives (LCO), Life Cycle Architecture (LCA) and Initial Operational Capability (IOC)" (Boehm 2000). At each of the anchor points, stakeholders will review the key artifacts of the stage.

Finally, invariant 6 states that besides the construction aspects, *the development process needs to focus also on the overall life cycle itself*. This means that long-term concerns should always be taken into account.

The spiral model has significant advantages over previously described models. The emphasis on risk analysis provides a major improvement and makes it an ideal model for large, mission-critical projects (Munassar and Govardhan 2010). On the downside, it is not very efficient in smaller projects; the risk assessment process can increase the expenses of the system to a degree where even making the system, regardless of risks, can be more financially sustainable. The risk assessment is also a procedure that demands a very peculiar expertise and needs to be custom-made for every system, which will contribute even further to a steep rise in costs (Rahmany 2012).

2.5 The V Life Cycle Model

The V-Model was presented in the final years of the 1980s by Paul Rook, as a variation over the waterfall model that attempted to emphasize the existing connection between each of the stages of the development process and its respective stage of tests. By focusing on this relationship, it ensures that adequate quality measurements and testing are constantly resorted to throughout the life cycle (Skidmore 2006).

The method thus presented is that each step is implemented by resorting to detailed documentation from the previous step. With this documentation, the product is checked and approved at each stage of the process, before it can move on to the next stage (Balaji and Murugaiyan 2012). With constant testing, and its respective documentation, it is possible to increase the overall efficiency of the process, particularly because eventual problems can be detected and resolved early (Mathur and Malik 2010) (Fig. 2.4).

The V-Model starts off with a very similar premise to the classic waterfall models. In successive steps, the project goes from analysis of requirements and specifications, to architectural and detailed design, to coding. However, instead of

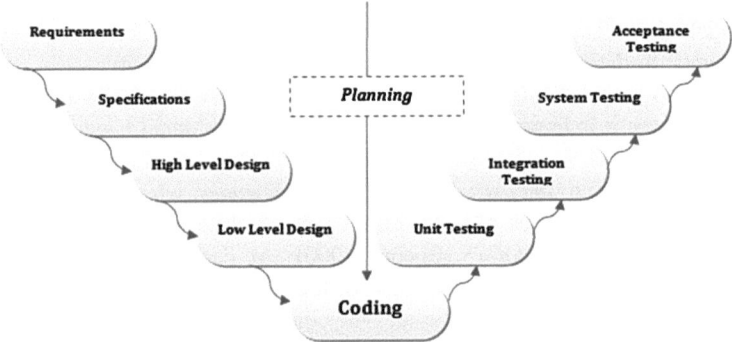

Fig. 2.4 V life cycle model (adapted from Balaji and Murugaiyan 2012)

continuing this downward ladder, there is a parallel structure that moves upward from the coding stage, giving the model its distinct V shape. The upward ladder describes each of the testing steps that follows coding, starting with unit testing and ending with acceptance testing, the final step before final release (Mathur and Malik 2010).

In that sense, the V-Model describes three successive layers of system development that can be described as requirements (overall system), high-level design (system architecture), and low-level design (software components). To each of these layers, there is a corresponding layer of planning and testing. Planning is, indeed, the axis that stands between the left and right ladders that compose the V, as it is the mediating action set between design and testing (Munassar and Govardhan 2010).

The core objective of the V life cycle model is to illustrate the importance of the relationship between development and testing tasks. Nonetheless, the success of a project is also determined by its maintenance structure. To accommodate this reality, Mathur and Malik (2010) proposed an expanded version of the V-Model, called the advanced V-Model, that incorporates both testing and maintenance activities into the life cycle. This adds a third structure, or "branch," to the model that reflects the introduction of testing mechanisms after the final product is released, so that proper quality measurement, troubleshooting, and general maintenance can be ensured.

Since the V-Model addresses its errors shortly after they are identified, it becomes less expensive to resolve them, which is perhaps the greatest advantage of using this model, specifically when compared to the classic waterfall model. Also, because testing is fractioned throughout the process, all the parties of the development are responsible for it. This also means that testing methods are adequate to each of the stages. Furthermore, the fact that tests are performed since the beginning of the process only increases its efficiency (Mathur and Malik 2010).

On the other hand, and much like the waterfall model, this model is very rigid and there is little room for flexible adaptation, particularly because any alteration in the requirements will render all existing documentation and testing obsolete. Since it requires a great deal of resources, it is clearly optimized for large projects within large organizations (Rahmany 2012).

2.6 Rapid Application Development

Originally conceptualized in the 1970s, the rapid application development model was substantially developed and formalized by James Martin in the early 1990s. As the name suggests, it is driven by the idea that existing life cycle models are simply too rigid to permit a fast project development; therefore, there is need for a framework that can account for fast delivery while still maintaining high-quality standards. It is grounded on the principle that step-by-step structured life cycles inevitably entail delays and errors, urging the need for an alternative methodology.

This issue became more relevant as businesses became increasingly competitive and IT needed to keep up. When deadlines are the main priority and the swiftness of software development is critical, RAD presents itself as a very plausible solution.

RAD comprises a set of tools and guidelines that facilitate short-time deployment, within a predefined time frame or "timebox." The product is not developed in successive steps until a final, complete delivery, but rather it evolves in successive increments, following the priorities that are established by business—not technical—necessities (Gottesdiener 1995). Some of these tools and guidelines include planning methods, data and process modeling, code generation, testing, and debugging (Agarwal et al. 2000).

It is important to note that both developers and customers are involved in all of the increments. However, teams are generally small, highly skilled, and highly disciplined. They are required to flexibly adapt to eventual changing requirements and feedback from customers. Nevertheless, it is crucial to strike the proper balance between flexibility and structural stability. Underlying models to the product's design are still necessary (Gottesdiener 1995), but not as rigid step-by-step guides to be followed to the letter (Fig. 2.5).

RAD methodologies can follow three-stage or four-stage cycles. "The four-stage cycle consists of requirements planning, user design, construction, and cutover, while in the three-stage cycle, requirements planning and user design are consolidated into one iterative activity" (Agarwal et al. 2000).

During planning, it is possible to analyze requirements, alternatives, and opportunities, as well as possible risks. This will form the basis for a definition of the project's goals and scope, and more importantly, it will allow for the establishment of the timebox, which is a fixed period during which a specific increment of the product is going to be developed. Each increment is then developed in a spiral-like model, through design, prototyping, and testing. This method essentially pushes the team closer to the project's business goals, by providing key deadlines that can be determined by market forces (Gottesdiener 1995).

While the advantages of the RAD are evident, due to its focus on swift delivery and effective developer–client communication, there are still a number of issues raised by this approach. One of the most obvious flaws is that it removes a great

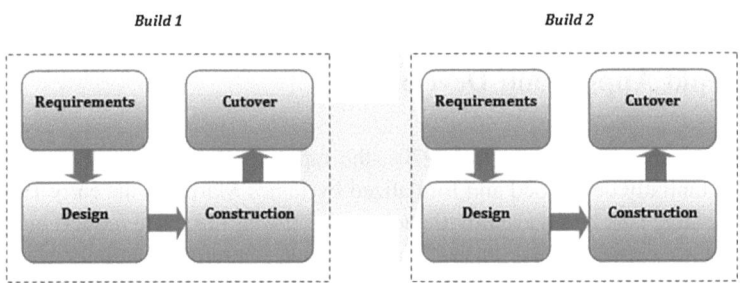

Fig. 2.5 Rapid application development entails a succession of increments or versions of the product, each built on a predetermined timebox and following a cycle of 4 (or 3) steps

deal of emphasis on minute planning and modeling at the start of the project, shifting that focus to the fluid process of system construction (Agarwal et al. 2000). Another prominent issue is that in faster development cycles, extensive quality testing will become less prioritized, reflecting in poorer quality overall, which means that effective RAD methodologies should reserve space for skilled individuals in quality control roles (Gottesdiener 1995). It is also possible that managers and leader have unrealistic expectations regarding the timeboxes, creating conflict with developing teams (Agarwal et al. 2000).

Thus, it is possible to assert that in order to be optimized, RAD life cycles must necessarily be balanced and be open to moderating agents.

2.7 Agile Life Cycle Model

With the popularization of waterfall-like SDLC models, an alternative approach has been developing that attempts to counter their rigidity and lack of flexibility. We have seen such examples in the incremental and RAD models. In 2001, the manifesto for agile software development was presented by 17 software developers, in a new attempt to bring together the best traits of other agile-like models into one framework. Since then, agile methods of development have become increasingly popular (Bhalerao et al. 2009).

There are 12 principles that guide agile development models, which were outlined in the Agile manifesto. These principles can be summed up as follows (Beck et al. 2001):

- Customer satisfaction is the highest priority;
- Change in requirements is welcomed, no longer an obstacle;
- Software is delivered regularly in consecutive releases;
- Motivated individuals are key to successful projects;
- Face-to-face conversation is paramount to successful collaboration;
- Working software is the measure of the project's progress;
- Sustainable development should be encouraged;
- Emphasis on technical and design quality;
- Simplicity should be favored;
- Self-organizing teams are the best form of project development;
- There should be regular discussions on team improvement.

There are numerous subvariations of the Agile model that follow these principles, with some examples being the scrum and XP models. However, even considering the variation in timescales or stage description, it is possible to determine the general path that an agile development process will take, outlined in four steps.

The first step is *project selection and approval*. During this stage, a team consisting of developers, managers, and customers establishes the scope, purpose, and requirements of the product. There is also a thorough analysis of different alternatives to accomplish the established goals, as well as risk assessment for each idea (Bhalerao et al. 2009).

The second step is *project initiation*. After the establishment of a coherent project with respective goals and scope, a working team is built, with the appropriate environment and tools, as well as the working architecture in which the system will be based. This too is discussed among all stakeholders. At this point, it is also adequate to establish working time frames and schedules (Ambler 2009).

The third step is *construction iterations*, with each iteration consisting of both planning and building. Developers release working software in successive increments that will accommodate the evolution of requirements as outlined by the various stakeholders. Close collaboration is therefore a fundamental aspect of this process, as the most effective method to ensure quality and to keep the project's priorities well defined. Extensive testing of each iteration is also paramount at this point (Ambler 2009).

The fourth and final step is *product release*. This stage encompasses two stages: First, final testing of the entire system is done, as well as any necessary final reworks and documentations. Next, the product is released, at which point training is provided to the users in order to maximize operational integration. The working team might maintain the project so as to allow for product improvement as well as user support (Bhalerao et al. 2009) (Fig. 2.6).

The Agile SDLC emerged from the ever-increasing need to match the speed at which IT evolves. What sets it apart is its dexterity in developing products at a great speed, with products being deliverable in the course of weeks instead of months. This is possible due to the model's emphasis on collaborative efforts and documentation (Executive Brief 2008).

Another advantage of the Agile model is that it is very flexible. It has been occasionally combined with other existing models. It has the capacity to deliver systems whose requirements go through constant changes while, at the same time, demanding strict time limits.

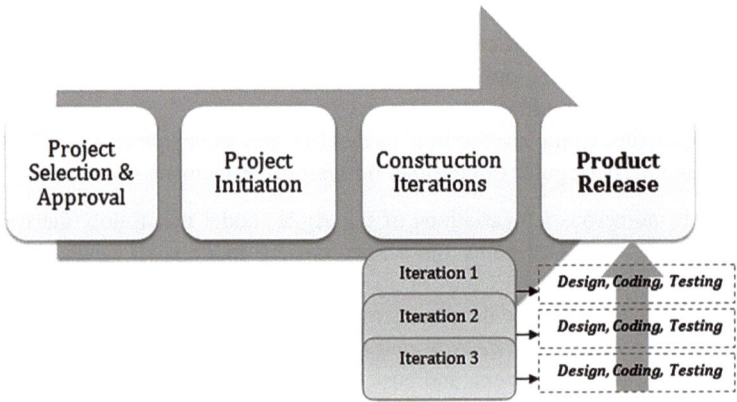

Fig. 2.6 An example of an Agile development life cycle

Finally, this model is often praised for its high degree of client satisfaction and user-friendliness, reduced error margins and the ability to incorporate solutions to address the needs of highly mutable requirements. Agile models are client-centric and advocate "short iterations and small releases" in order to obtain feedback on what has been accomplished. With the feedback that is received, improvements can be made that will have positive repercussions on the quality of the end product (Bhalerao et al. 2009).

2.8 The Prototyping Model

The prototyping model is an iterative framework that is at the center of many of the more agile approaches to software development, ever since the early 1980s, which lead to it being described in some studies as a specific model in itself. In 1997, Carr and Verner observed that in the past research, the SDLC models that adopted prototyping were found to be more dynamic and more responsive to client needs, as well as less risky and more efficient. For that reason, they attempted to summarize prototyping models in one consistent framework.

The prototyping model is based on the idea of creating the entirety or part of a system in a pilot version, called the prototype. It can be viewed as a process, either one that is part of the larger SDLC or the central approach that defines the SDLC in itself. The goal is ultimately to build in various versions and consistently refine those versions until a final product is reached (Carr and Verner 1997). The emphasis is placed on the creation of the software, with less attention to documentation. It is also a user-centric approach, because user feedback is fundamental to develop subsequent prototypes and, eventually, the final product (Sabale and Dani 2012) (Fig. 2.7).

A prototyping model essentially entails four different stages. First, user's requirements and needs are analyzed and identified. Next, the team will develop a

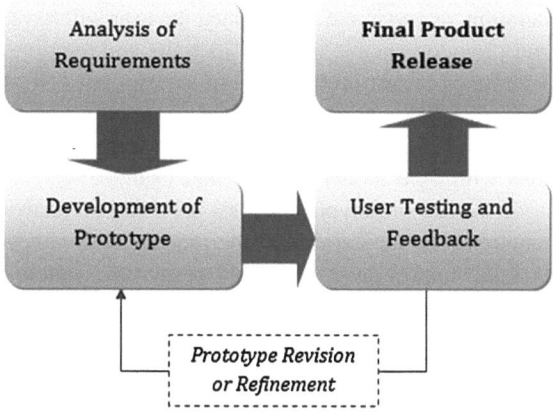

Fig. 2.7 The prototype model (adapted from Carr and Verner 1997)

working prototype of the product, which is then implemented so that the users can test it and provide real-time feedback and experience. If improvements and changes are found necessary, the prototype is revised and refined, and a new prototype is released and implemented for testing. This subcycle will go on until the product is generally accepted by the users and no longer requires substantial changes or updates, at which time the final version is released (Carr and Verner 1997).

There are various types of prototyping, according to specific needs of the project. These can be summarized in three categories: exploration, experimentation, and evolution (Floyd 1984).

The *exploratory approach* is centered on the premise that requirements are thoroughly explored with each iteration. Under this category, we find rapid throwaway prototyping, essentially a method of delivering fast releases of the product with each iteration, exploring needs and requirements with each version, and perfecting the next version accordingly. Needs are assessed as the product is used and tested. On the other hand, the spiral model, which we have previously discussed, is another form of exploratory prototyping, where prototypes are employed in successive stages of the development process, each following the waterfall pattern (Carr and Verner 1997).

The *experimental approach* entails that a solution to the user's needs is first proposed and then evaluated through experimental use. The use of simulation programs and skeleton programming (delivering only the most essential features of the system so the user can get a general idea of what the final product will be like) falls under this category, but there are many other examples, as it is the most common form of prototyping (Floyd 1984).

Finally, the *evolutionary approach* essentially describes development in successive versions and is closest to incremental and iterative life cycle models, in that its main goal is to accommodate the eventual changes in requirements and needs. The prototype is used fundamentally to allow for easier contact with the product, in order to pinpoint perceived needs. Each prototype is no more than a version of the product, and each version serves as the prototype for the next one (Floyd 1984).

By using a form of the prototyping model, a development project can easily adapt to changing requirements, because there is constant feedback. With each iteration, or version of the product, the user will have the ability to test the prototype and provide valuable input on its traits and requirements. This provides the model with much higher probabilities of success, as well as low risks. On the other hand, because there is not much emphasis on extensive documentation, and the product evolves as it is created, the time frame for the development project is much shorter than with rigid models (Sabale and Dani 2012).

However, prototyping models are weak on analysis and design planning. While requirements are assessed as the product is developed in successive versions, there is little control over costs and resources, which can dramatically increase the financial cost of the project (Sabale and Dani 2012). Therefore, we can conclude that prototyping is ideal for larger projects and particularly for user-centric ones.

2.9 Usability Engineering Life Cycle

Usability engineering is a concept of software engineering that places usability characteristics at the center of the development process and implies that constant measurements and analysis of usability should be undertaken as the development proceeds. It is primarily related to user interface design. As a model for SDLC, it was originally proposed by Deborah Mayhew in the late 1990s.

The main objective of usability engineering is to apply structured iterative design and evaluation to all stages of the SDLC, thus ensuring constant involvement of the user within the process. The life cycle is segmented in three parts—analysis/design, development, and evaluation. Across the three sections, the successive activities are performed, in a waterfall-like process, but reflecting the existence of various iterations before the final product is released (Gabbard et al. 2003).

Crucial to this process is determining who will constitute the product's user base and what will they be doing with the product. User task analysis is the central activity at the beginning of the process and can be achieved through surveys, interviews, observation, etc. The product of such analysis consists of scenarios, potentialities, and requirements that will be taken into account for the next stages of the process. After establishing the requirements and defining them through user-centered metrics, an initial design is outlined and swiftly prototyped, so that it can be followed by extensive usability evaluation and testing (Gabbard et al. 2003).

This life cycle model is evidently user-centric, as it intends to create a system that is financially effective but also presents very high usability. The fact that it helps the development of systems that are extremely user-friendly prevents errors that derive from human misuse of the interface. Consequently, it promotes high productivity.

When considering the entirety of the life of the interface, this development life cycle, because it diminishes the need for the addition of features at a stage of the development when they have an increased cost, has the potential to decrease expenses (Gabbard et al. 2003)

2.10 The Star Life Cycle Model

The star life cycle model was proposed by Harton and Hix in the late 1980s, as the result of extensive observation of developers in real-time environments (Helms 2001). It is a particular variant of usability engineering, a user-centric set of software development guidelines, and thus rejects the rigid, step-by-step nature of waterfall-like models.

The most innovative premise is that each step in development does not necessarily fall in a fixed position within a fixed process. Instead, it is assumed that there are a number of essential stages of development, but they can be processed in various orders and various time frames, according to the specific needs of the

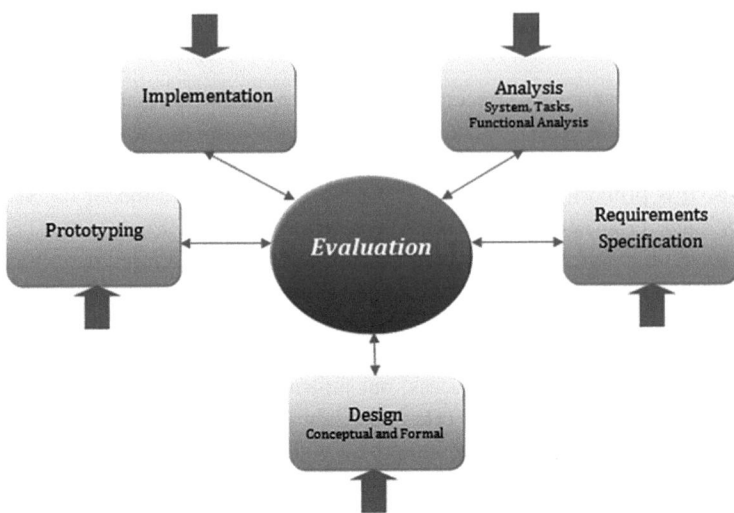

Fig. 2.8 The star life cycle model (adapted from Stone et al. 2005)

project, with the possibility of going back over a given stage numerous times or completely skipping another stage if it proves irrelevant. Thus, for example, a developer might start by experimenting with various design options and, in that process, learning more specific requirements of the project (Helms 2001).

The fundamental rule behind this premise is that each stage must be accompanied by extensive evaluation. All the stages are interrelated, and in the development process, it is possible to shift to any of them at any point, just as long as that stage is evaluated. Likewise, each action that is completed, regardless of its order, has to be thoroughly analyzed. This includes extensive testing and data collection on that particular activity, through such methods as interviewing users or observing their use of the system within the working context (Stone et al. 2005) (Fig. 2.8).

Users are positioned at the center of the development cycle and are encouraged to participate in any of the stages: at the beginning of the process, to help establish the system's requirements and define their goals and needs; during prototyping, to ensure thorough testing under working conditions; before final release, again to provide extensive testing; and after the system's delivery, to monitor any possible issues and communicate their overall experience with the system (Stone et al. 2005). This perspective clearly derives from the star model's close relationship with user interface design, as it was originally conceived within that particular context.

The model is laid out like a star, hence its name. Evaluation is at the center of the star, since it is the fundamental premise that will guide all other steps. Around the central step, we find the different possible stages of development; however, they are not connected to each other. This does not mean that there is no relationship between the different stages; what it does illustrate is that every step is interconnected through the process of evaluation (Helms 2001).

2.11 Hybrid System Development Life Cycles

An environment of increasing competitiveness demands systems that are safe and trustworthy. They also have to be adaptable and flexible to the changes that can happen at any moment, in a fast paced, ever-evolving world. This brings complications for the development process. A common response to these issues is the combination of different system development life cycles.

SDLC models each have their own peculiar characteristics, which can be both advantageous and detrimental, depending on the type of project requirements and features. Once a project is hypothesized, a model is chosen to fit its purposes. But if the particular characteristics of the project do not necessarily fit one specific model, it is possible to combine guidelines from more than one. This combination is primarily done to harness the qualities of a model and reduce its weaknesses by incorporating the strengths of another model (Rahmany 2012).

An example of combined life cycle models is the case of a development process that is being guided by the spiral model, but that later in the process demands a change in the requirements. To accommodate this need, the agile model could be incorporated (Rahmany 2012).

Madachy et al. (2006) have outlined a hybrid SDLC model which they named the scalable spiral model. The main purpose was to combine a plan-driven approach with an agile one. Development is organized into thoroughly planned increments, which take into consideration relatively stable, initial requirements. However, upon the release of each increment, it is crucial to have an agile team focusing on market, competition, and technological analysis, as well as user feedback and renegotiation of the characteristics of the next increments. The model ultimately aims at simultaneously catering for the challenges of rapid change and the need for risk management and dependability (Madachy et al. 2006).

Munassar and Govardhan (2010) have also attempted a similar approach, which they simply named the hybrid model. They picked up essential traits from such different models as waterfall, iteration, V-shaped, spiral, and extreme programming (XP). It consists of a series of seven steps that are interconnected with each other: planning, requirements (at which point risk analysis is undertaken), design, implementation (including testing), integration development, deployment, and maintenance. Although the process appears to be outlined in the same style of a waterfall approach, the relationship between the different stages is fluid and multidirectional, accounting for possible changes in requirements and the need to revise design features after testing. The authors argue that this approach would permit to combine the best characteristics of each model: It promotes good habits of define-before-design and design-before-code (like the waterfall model), while, at the same time, it avoids the dangers of rigid development by introducing early testing. It is also iterative, but still incorporates risk analysis, and the test-based approach allows for high usability (Munassar and Govardhan 2010).

2.12 Conclusion

Variety in SDLC models and frameworks is great. We have discussed the most prominent ones, but there are numerous other models, many of them hybrid in nature and designed to respond to specific needs of specific projects or simply to attempt a flawless approach by combining various models and reducing their individual weaknesses. This great variety means that the process of choosing which model to adopt for a particular development project can be complicated. Nevertheless, there are certain fundamental aspects of the project that can facilitate the decision.

The requirements of the system play a key role. If requirements are strict and immutable, the team might adopt a waterfall approach, but if requirements are expected to change often, or are not clearly defined at the start, the team will probably adopt a more agile and/or iterative approach.

The deadline for the development of the system is also an important factor. It is clear that if the schedule is tighter, a rigid step-by-step model based on extensive documentation and late testing would be unreasonably slow, thus excluding waterfall models.

The project's dimension is one of the most influential factors. The larger the project, the more rigid the model tends to be, because a large team comprised of many developers makes agile responses more complicated. The location of the teams is also a factor: If the teams involved in the project are geographically dispersed, a waterfall-like model is probably the best approach, for the clarity of its stages and tasks. An agile development, where tight communication is important, is an approach that is more beneficial to small teams working closer together.

Finally, resources should always be taken into account. Projects that involve intricate dynamics and demand the use of peculiar expertise and technology are easier to accomplish with models of strict planning, such as the waterfall (Executive Brief 2008).

Choosing the right model for a project is a crucial step of system development, so as IS continues to be fundamental to modern business and organizational contexts, SDLC models will continue to be developed, researched, and utilized.

References

Agarwal, R., Prasad, J., Tanniru, M., & Lynch, J. (2000). Risks of rapid application development. *Communications of the ACM, 43*(11), 177–188.

Ambler, S. (2009). The Agile system development life cycle (SDLC). Retrieved from http://www.ambysoft.com/essays/agileLifecycle.html

Balaji, S., Murugaiyan, M., (2012). Waterfall vs. V-Model vs. Agile: A comparative study on SDLC. *International Journal of Information Technology and Business Management 2*(1), 26–30.

Beck, K., Beedle, M., Van Bennekum, A., Cockburn, A., Cunningham, W., Fowler, M., Grenning, J., Highsmith, J., Hunt, A., Jeffries, R., Kern, J., Marick, B., Martin, R., Mellor, S., Schwaber,

References

K., Sutherland, J., & Thomas, D. (2001). Manifesto for Agile software development. Retrieved from http://agilemanifesto.org

Bhalerao, S., Puntambekar, D., & Ingle, M. (2009). Generalizing Agile software development life cycle. *International Journal on Computer Science and Engineering, 1*(3), 222–226.

Boehm, B. (1988). A Spiral model of software development and enhancement. *IEEE Computer, May 1988*, pp. 61–72.

Boehm, B. (2000). Spiral development: experience, principles and refinements (Special Report CMU/SEI-2000-SR-008). Carnegie Mellon University.

Carr, M., & Verner, J. (1997). Prototyping and software development approaches. Department of Information Systems, Hong Kong: City University of Hong Kong.

Cockburn, A. (2008). Using both incremental and iterative development. *STSC Cross Talk, 21*(5), 27–30.

Cohen, S., Dori, D., & de Uzi Haan, A. (2010). A software system development Life Cycle model for improved stakeholders' communication and collaboration. *International Journal of Computers Communications & Control, 1*, 23–44.

Stone, D., Jarrett, C., Woodroffe, M., & Minocha, S. (2005). Introducing user interface design. In D. Stone, C. Jarrett, M. Woodroffe, & S. Minocha (Eds.), *User interface design and evaluation* (pp. 3–24). San Francisco: Elsevier.

Durrani, Q. S., & Qureshi, S. A. (2012). Usability engineering practices in SDLC. *Proceedings of the 2012 International Conference on Communications and Information Technology (ICCT)* (pp. 319–324).

Executive Brief (2008). *Which Life Cycle is best for your project?* Retrieved from http://www.executivebrief.com

Floyd, C. (1984). A systematic look at prototyping. In R. Budde, K. Kuhlenkamp, L. Mathiassen, & H. Züllighoven (Eds.), *Approaches to Prototyping* (pp. 1–18). Berlin: Springer.

Gabbard, J., Hix, D., Swan, E., Livingston, M., Hollerer, T., Julier, S., Brown, D., & Baillot, Y. (2003). Usability engineering for complex interactive systems development. *Proceedings of Human Systems Integration Symposium 2003, Engineering for Usability* (pp. 1–13).

Gottesdiener, E. (1995). RAD realities: beyond the hype to how RAD really works. *Application Development Trends, August 1995* (pp. 28–38).

Helms, J. (2001). Developing and evaluating the (LUCID/Star)*Usability Engineering Process Model (Master's thesis). Retrieved from http://scholar.lib.vt.edu/theses/available/etd-05102001-190814/unrestricted/jhelmsthesisnew.pdf

Jirava, P. (2004). System development life cycle. In *Scientific Papers of the University of Pardubice Series D.* (pp. 118–125). Pardubice: Univerzita Pardubice.

Madachy, R., Boehm, B., & Lane, J. (2006). Spiral lifecycle increment modeling for new hybrid processes. In Q. Wang, D. Pfahl, D. Raffo, & P. Wernick (Eds.), *Software process change* (pp. 167–177). Berlin: Springer.

Massey, V., & Satao, K. (2012). Comparing various SDLC models and the new proposed model on the basis of available methodology. *International Journal of Advanced Research in Computer Science and Software Engineering, 2*(4), 170–177.

Mathur, S., & Malik, S. (2010). Advancements in the V-Model. *International Journal of Computer Applications IJCA, 1*(12), 30–35.

Munassar, N., & Govardhan, A. (2010a). Comparison between five models of software engineering. *International Journal of Computer Science Issues, 7*(5), 94–101.

Munassar, N., & Govardhan, A. (2010b). Hybrid model for software development processes. *Proceedings of the 11th International Arab Conference on Information Technology.*

Rahmany, N. (2012). The differences between life cycle models—Advantages and disadvantages. Retrieved from http://narbit.wordpress.com/2012/06/10/the-differences-between-life-cycle-models-advantages-and-disadvantages/

Royce, W. (1970). Managing the development of large software systems. *Proceedings of IEEE WESCON* (pp. 1–9).

Sabale, R., & Dani, A. (2012). Comparative study of prototype model for software engineering with system development Life Cycle. *IOSR Journal of Engineering, 2*(7), 21–24.

Skidmore, S. (2006). The V-Model. *Student Accountant, January 2006* (pp. 48–49).
Tetlay, A., & John, P. (2009). Determining the lines of system maturity, system readiness and capability readiness in the system development lifecycle. Presented at the 7th Annual Conference on Systems Engineering Research (CSER09), Loughborough University.
Texas Project Delivery Framework, U.S. Department of Information Resources (2008). System development Life Cycle guide. Texas Department of Information Resources. Retrieved from http://www.dir.texas.gov/SiteCollectionDocuments/IT%20Leadership/Framework/Framework%20Extensions/SDLC/SDLC_guide.pdf
Tilloo, R. (2013). What is incremental model in software engineering? Retrieved from http://www.technotrice.com/incremental-model-in-software-engineering

Chapter 3
Information Systems Development Methodologies

3.1 Introduction

An information system (IS) is commonly known as a system whose central element is information. Its main purpose is to store, treat, and provide information with the intention to support specific functions or processes within an organization. In this context, information systems development methodologies (ISDMs) are used by entities to better organize the IS development process (Zaied et al. 2003) and also to efficiently identify the key elements and stages of an IS developing process. The main purpose of the ISDMs is to aid in the better development of an information system within a specific organization.

Information systems are implemented within an organization with the sole purpose of improving the effectiveness and efficiency of that organization (Hevner et al. 2004). In general, their main goal is to ensure agility in the communication of information, as well as the quality of the information, because efficient communication is mandatory in any well-organized corporation.

In the last decades, with the exponential growth of the information society, we have seen an expansion of theory and concepts regarding IS. Thus, a multitude of models and methodologies was defined and studied, with the purpose of establishing ideal methods of IS development. Gasson (1995) states that "a methodology is more than just a method (the 'how' of information systems development, ISD), or a process-model. A methodology is a holistic approach: it embodies an analytical framework which is conveyed through intersubjective representational practices and operationalized through a 'toolbox' of analytical methods, tools and techniques. Underlying the analytical framework is a process-model which indicates the sequence and relative duration of development activities" (p. 2). The concept of methodology, in this context, is the framework that contains all the methods, actions, and processes used in the development of an information system.

With this concept of methodology in mind, we will list and analyze some of the most well-known ISDMs that have been established in existing literature.

3.2 Information Systems Development Methodologies

3.2.1 Agile Methodology

The use of agile methods has rapidly increased among the ISD arena, a swift evolution that has been almost entirely determined by practitioners rather than researchers (Conboy 2009). Although its fundamental principles have been around since the 1970s, agile methodology has truly gained momentum during the last 15 years (Abbas et al. 2008). As agile methods became increasingly popular, researchers have been more and more interested in studying and systematizing them (Conboy 2009).

Agile methodologies have evolved around the concept that the development of IS is a creative work, where design activities occupy a key position (Tumbas and Matkovic 2006); on the other hand, they are also based on the premise that the development process often involves constant changes and adaptations that give rise to a need for flexible approaches and methods. It can thus be asserted that the increased use of agile methods is connected to the instability of the technological environment. Customers are not always able to describe their necessities, in a comprehensive manner, at the beginning of a specific project; therefore, developers found it necessary to create methods that are capable of adapting to changing circumstances and specifications along the design and development process. According to Tumbas and Matkovic (2006), the development of IS processes needs to be flexible in order to allow its users to analyze and adjust their needs and requirements frequently, without endangering the effectiveness of the entire process. Agile methods aim at responding directly to this necessity.

Additionally, it is argued that agile methods have emerged as a reaction to the incapacity of previous methods to rapidly and efficiently stand up to dynamic and changing contexts (Abrahamsson et al. 2009 citing Highsmith 2002), which are common place in the context of IS and information society.

Within this context, Conboy (2009) defines agility as a method's continued predisposition to rapidly or inherently create change, proactively or reactively embrace change and learn from it, while at the same time contributing to the customer's perception of value. For Abbas et al. (2008), an agile method is adaptive (this method can handle change, in technology and requirements, even to the point of changing the method itself), iterative, and incremental (with every iteration, part the system is developed, tested, and improved, while a new part is being developed), and people-oriented (it highlights face-to-face communication within the team and with the customer, who is closely involved with the development process). Furthermore, to ensure effective development, agile methods stress informal communication and require frequent feedback through reviews and evaluations in collaboration with customers on-site (Paelke and Nebe 2008).

Thus, it can be summarized that agile methods are primarily adaptive rather than predictable, while also aiming at faster development times and more integration with customer needs. The major advantage of these methods is that they can easily adjust to different project steps (Aydin et al. 2004), making them easily adaptable to the great variety of specifications that different projects might present. This is one explanation as to why the agile methodology has become so popular.

An example of agile methodology is extreme programming (XP), an iterative method of software development that requires maximum customer interaction. The development cycle is divided into shorter cycles. Each cycle starts with the collection of user requirements, followed by iteration planning, where the number of cycles and respective timeframes are established. The product is then developed, usually through pair programming. The resulting version of the product is tested, both technically as well as for acceptance among the users. The feedback taken from this testing and customer intervention is taken into account for the development of the next version, thus starting the next cycle. This method is repeated until a version is built that is acceptable for the majority of users, managers, and developers alike (Sharma et al. 2012).

Scrum is a similar method, particularly designed for optimum development time and customer satisfaction. Each iteration of the development process is called a "sprint," and it is established that the maximum duration for each sprint is 30 days. After collecting user requirements, they are prioritized through a list called the "product backlog," followed by careful planning of the perceived necessary sprints to achieve it, and what will constitute the focus of each sprint. This is the "sprint backlog." During the actual development in each sprint phase, there are daily meetings to discuss the progress so far and exchange feedback and experiences. It is important to note that with each sprint, a working version of the software is produced. It will be subsequently improved and completed with the next sprints (Sharma et al. 2012).

In a 2013 survey on North American and European companies, the Scrum method was concluded to be the most commonly adopted agile methodology in the course of that year, followed by Scrum/XP hybrid methods, overall making up for 73 % of the total agile methodologies used in the survey's context (VersionOne 2013). This is indicative of how flexible the Scrum method is.

3.2.2 Structured Systems Analysis and Design Methodology (SSADM)

The Structured Systems Analysis and Design Methodology (known as SSADM) was primarily used by government departments, since it is conceived for large-scale information systems (Schumacher 2001). It originally developed as a framework for systems analysis and design to be adopted by the British Central Computer and Telecommunications Agency in the late 1980s (Edwards et al. 1989).

In spite of being created for large-scale information systems, it is argued that SSADM can be used to develop projects of all sizes (Edwards et al. 1989), making it an alternative approach to agile methods. The two main characteristics of this methodology is the splitting of the system into smaller parts, in order to establish the order and the interaction between the different stages, and the usage of modeling methods and diagrams to present a more structured and logical definition to users and developers (Manteghi and Jahromi 2012). With this structured and analytical system, it is possible to decompose the system into small units, with the purpose of defining the meaning, order, and connections between the various units that compose a large-scale information system.

A typical SSAD method will be divided into a maximum of 8 stages. The first is strategic planning, where an analysis of the current environment is undertaken, along with a discussion and establishment of the plan and scope of the project. This is followed by a *feasibility study* that aims at determining if the project is technically, financially and socially viable, as well as how it fits within the organization's culture and goals. Next, there is a thorough *analysis and specification of requirements*, where current systems and respective problems are evaluated, and what is necessary for a new system to address existing issues and necessities. This information is collected by a variety of methods, including surveys and observation as well as resorting to existing studies. The next stage is *logical system specification*, where according to the requirements found in the previous stage, a set of technical solutions is established. At this point, the planned system is more specific and to-the-point. Thus, it is followed by *physical design*, where the logical system is given from through program specifications, database definitions, etc. The next stage is *construction and testing*, when the actual programming and assembly takes place. *Transition* entails the process of moving from an old system to the newly built system. Finally, the last stage involves *production, maintenance, and review*. The new system is established, and after its implementation, its success and adequacy is measured for further studies and alterations (Goodland and Riha 1999).

The SSADM deals primarily with three data-oriented views, namely logical data structures (LDS), data flow diagrams, and entity life histories (ELHs) that demonstrate how organizations change over time (Avison and Taylor 1997). However, a closer look at the related literature reveals that there are ten specific SSADM techniques. These are (Edwards et al. 1989) as follows:

- Data flow diagrams (DFDs)
- Logical data structures (LDS)
- Entity life histories (ELHs)
- Relational data analysis/third normal form (RDA/TNF)
- Composite logical data design (CLDD)
- Process outlines (POs)
- Logical dialogue outlines (LDOs)
- First cut data design (DD)
- First cut programs (PROG)
- Physical design control (PDC)

Besides the techniques listed above, Ashworth (1988) presents several basic principles regarding this methodology (see Table 3.1).

3.2 Information Systems Development Methodologies

Table 3.1 Principles of SSADM

Differentiation between logical and physical	SSADM makes a distinction between designing the logical basis of the system, and designing its physical properties
Diverse views of the system	Specific attention to the logical structure of the data, how that data flows in and out of the system and how it is changed (entity life histories)
Top-down and bottom-up	Top-down procedures (data flow diagramming, logical data structuring), and bottom-up approaches (relational data analysis)
User involvement	It is paramount that end users participate in the development of the system from the beginning
Quality assurance	Quality reviews must be performed at the end of each stage of the process, by users, developers and experts outside of the project
Self-documentation	Each stage must be accompanied by extensive documentation, so that records on the progress and outcome of the project are always updated

It is crucial that the aforementioned principles stand to support the entire development project (Ashworth 1988). These principles should be seen as guidelines that must be followed when adapting this method to specific environments and contexts.

Schumacher (2001) argues that SSADM is primarily focused on the design stages of the process. It is evident that both planning and design are paramount to this process. Its basic, fundamental idea is that if planning and design are thorough and adequate to the requirements of the project, then the probability of the project failing is lower. Therefore, it can be asserted that SSADM is a much more rigid perspective than the agile methodology, because of the amount of time and resources spent on planning and analysis, as well as the importance of documentation as opposed to face-to-face communication. However, the fact that user involvement is a crucial factor means that there is openness for user feedback along the project, primarily at the testing phase.

3.2.3 Soft Systems Methodology (SSM)

The soft systems methodology (SSM) emerged in the late 1960s and was popularized when Checkland and his colleagues at Lancaster University questioned the usage of hard systems thinking in real-life contexts and situations (Hardman et al. 2011). It is fundamentally based on the distinction between "hard" and "soft" thinking. "Hard thinking" implies a form of observation of the world, where specific aspects are identified as organized systems that can be analyzed or engineered. "Soft thinking" implies viewing the world as a set of disorganized, confusing, and complex realities that can be organized by the viewer in systems to facilitate analysis (Checkland 2000). Thus, SSM is a specific approach that starts off with the assumption that a system is not a real entity, but rather a construction of the human mind. It's assumed that there are many different perspectives on what a given system is, which will be taken into account as the system is analyzed or built.

SSM is a systemic methodology, essentially created to face problem situations of a complex nature with several important aspects, actors, and points of view (Sánchez and Meija 2008). In this sense, the SSM proposes a variety of views of the problematic situation, from the perspective of each participant in the process, in order to reach a compromise between each different participant's point of view, building a bridge between them. Given that it is an action research methodology, SSM provides not just a guide to intervention in complex situations, but also the feedback to promote knowledge gains from that intervention (Tajino et al. 2005). Although soft thinking can be used in any context, it is primarily used for analysis and problem solving in intricate and disorganized environments.

This methodology allows the clarification of confusing and problematic situations by supporting thinking in layers, where the starting point must be the search for the crucial "core purpose" motivating the organization (Checkland 2000). Patel (1995) states that its application is not limited to technologically based organizations, as its focus on human activity systems means that SSM is likely capable to address all areas where human involvement is prominent. Human activity systems, in this context, consist of a series of activities associated together in a logical manner to represent a determined whole (Tajino et al. 2005).

Generally, there are seven clear stages to a soft systems approach (Sánchez and Meija 2008), illustrated in Fig. 3.1.

Stages one and two correspond to the definition of the situation and/or problem. In stage three, we leave the real world and we enter the in the system environment, and thus, we arrive to stage four that is related to the development of the model. After the development of the models, we return to the real world in stage five, six, and seven in order to compare the models to reality, create solutions to problems that might appear when comparing the model to real-life situations and lastly implement the model.

Fig. 3.1 Stages of SSM

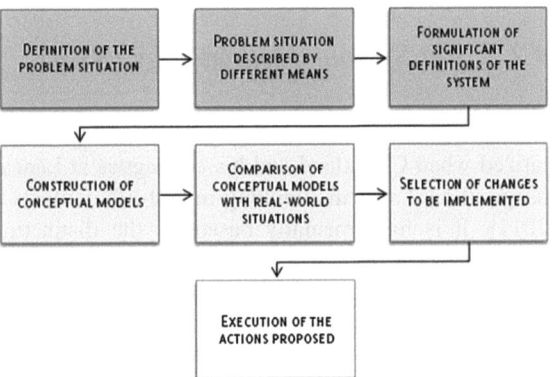

Rodríguez-Ulloa et al. (2011) state that the aim of SSM is to organize and establish practical changes in sociocultural systems in which the traditional methods were unable to distinguish and consider "soft" variables that, in the most cases, describe the course of action for organizations (such as "political factors," "power influence," "culture," "ideology," and "values") and consequently, SSM is particularly useful to search for feasible solutions to soft problems in social issues.

By using systems thinking in analysis, SSM has the ability to identify difficulties and pinpoint the real source of a given problem, by looking at the organization as a whole, but also by looking at each of the organization's elements and their influence and approach over the central issue.

Within the context of information systems, this methodology primarily evolved from the need to understand other factors and problems that can affect the design and development of an IS. It allows for a more comprehensive understanding of the variables that can influence IS, combining both the technical and the external factors. It perceives the significance of cultural and social values of individuals and groups within an organization, which can originate a multiplicity of insights (Savage and Mingers 1996). Savage and Mingers (1996) also argue that SSM could be of valuable assistance in improving the perception of user requirements, because this methodology clearly allows for users to participate in the process and lend their own perspective and viewpoint, which will have its own impact on the conceptual model.

3.2.4 User-centered Development Methodology

A growing concern with user satisfaction lead to the popularization of user-centered development methodology, or user-centered design (UCD), a methodology that places the user at the core of the development process and, more importantly, makes the user an active component of that process. Gould and Lewis (1985) were pioneers in this approach. They argued that "any system designed for people to use should be easy to learn (and remember)," which lead to their consideration of three fundamental principles for user-centered methods: *early focus on users and tasks, empirical measurement, and iterative design* (Gould and Lewis 1985).

Essentially, their work focused on usability as a form of evaluation of the system's adequacy. Because often the perspective of the user can be merely hypothesized by the development team, based on stereotypes or generic expectations, Gould and Lewis proposed the importance of bringing the user into direct contact with the development team, to ensure that realistic user requirements and needs were properly introduced into the system's creation. Likewise, the authors observe that a truly user-centered methodology interprets the testing and prototyping stages as usability assessments, and not marketing opportunities: the user should be able to test the product without being convinced or talked into accepting it (Wallach and Scholz 2012).

UCD, as defined by Mao et al. (2005), is a "multidisciplinary design approach based on the active involvement of users to improve the understanding of user and task requirements, and the iteration of design and evaluation." A user-centered methodology includes methods and approaches that provide the user with a key role. It is argued that it essentially focuses on usability throughout all the development process (Gulliksen et al. 2003).

Each information system brings together different users with individual differences and experiences. These individual differences and experiences among users can have a determining impact and lasting influence over the system's performance; thus, it is crucial in UCD to combine users with systems configurations in order to optimize and improve their performance (Allen 2000).

In IS, the differences between users must be seen as a benefit to the design of a system. By considering those differences, it is possible to design a more complete system that can reach a wider range of users, making that particular system more flexible and more useful in different contexts and environments.

In Gulliksen et al. (2003), it is proposed that there are twelve principles for UCD design, summarized in Table 3.2.

Table 3.2 Principles of user-centered system design

User focus	The goals of the activity, the work domain, or context of use, the users' goals, tasks, and needs should guide the development from the beginning
Active user involvement	Representative users should actively participate, early, and continuously throughout the entire development process and throughout the system lifecycle
Evolutionary system development	Development should be both iterative and incremental
Simple design representations	The design must be represented in such ways that it can be easily understood by users and all stakeholders
Prototyping	Early and continuously, prototypes should be used to visualize and evaluate ideas and design solutions in cooperation with end users
Evaluate use in context	Baseline usability goals and design criteria should control the development
Explicit and conscious design activities	The development process should contain dedicated design activities
A professional attitude	The development process should be performed by effective multidisciplinary teams
Usability champion	Usability experts should be involved early and continuously throughout the development lifecycle
Holistic design	All aspects that influence the future use situation should be developed in parallel
Process customization	The UCD process must be specific, adapted, and/or implemented locally in each organization
A user-centered attitude	UCD requires a user-centered attitude throughout the project team, the development organization, and the client organization

Source Gulliksen et al. (2003)

The UCD is accomplished when "every phase of the product lifecycle follows the principles of user-centered design, when UCD team is provided with the proper skills and experience, it is supported by the management commitment and a proper UCD infrastructure and when awareness and culture are properly disseminated in and out of the organization" (Venturi and Troost 2004).

Following this description, we can assert that it is not sufficient to have the user participate in a given stage of the development process, but rather, a user-centered approach and mentality must be present in every stage of the design of a specific project or organization. It is a methodology that combines user participation with a formative assessment; thus, it is primarily based on a multidisciplinary team, the interaction between the user and system, the active involvement of users and a strong user-centered infrastructure.

UCD methods are generally believed to have improved IS development, product value, and usability, even though the degree to which UCD methods are adopted varies greatly between organizations (Vredenburg et al. 2002).

3.2.5 ETHICS Methodology

The Effective Technical and Human Implementation of Computer-based Systems methodology (known as ETHICS), originally conceived by Professor Enid Mumford in the 1970s, is a "problem-solving methodology aimed at identifying cause–effect interactions for solving problems" (Adman and Warren 2000). Its ultimate goal is to strike an ideal balance between the social and technical perspectives within a given system or product. Thus, it is heavily focused on the combination between technical factors (usability, efficiency, adequacy…) with human factors (user needs, job satisfaction, cultural context…), bringing together hard and soft thinking. However, the ETHICS methodology implies that specific analysis of both perspectives is required before they can be brought together into a common approach (Adman and Warren 2000). This approach is referred to as the socio-technical perspective, and it is the essential component of the methodology.

The ETHICS methodology was originally created as a guide to user participation in system design (Wong and Tate 1994) and, as such, it considers users' knowledge and skills as vital aspects for the successful development of a system. It presents four central aspects that form user participation: *structure* (concerned both with direct and indirect forms of participation within a complex organization), *content* (engages the consideration of what subjects are to be determined), *process* (integrity issues are considered), and *obstacles* (these include lack of trust, conflicts of interest, time pressures and stress, low morale, effects of authority, and communication gaps). Thus, user participation is fundamental in the ETHICS approach (Hirschheim and Klein 1994).

Fig. 3.2 ETHICS six-stage design

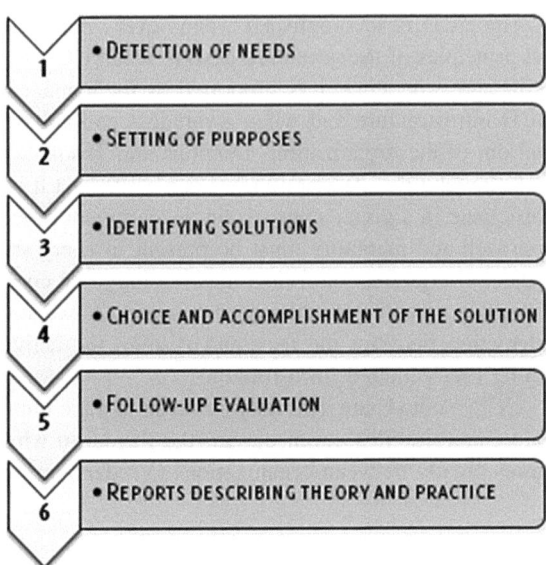

According to Mumford (1993), the ETHICS approach has three core purposes:

- To allow future users to have a more active role in the system development and consequently to accept more responsibility for designing the work structure that involves the technology. Here, it is present a user participation and sociotechnical approach;
- To guarantee that new systems are adequate to the users because it is necessary to ensure user efficiency and approval;
- To support users to become increasingly competent in the management of the system, therefore creating a shared activity with technical specialists, thus minimizing the demand of technical sources.

Mumford (2000) presents a summary of ETHICS as a six-stage framework (as shown in Fig. 3.2), but the use of these stages can differ according to the requirements and needs of specific projects and situations.

Since not all situations are the same, and there are different demands and purposes to different projects, the methodology must be adapted and used in accordance with the context in which it is included. The stages presented above should be used as guidelines to help the researcher/developer to assess if his/her course of action is strong and the most suitable to validate his/her system design. But these stages cannot be seen as rigid rules. The researcher/developer has to bear in mind the goals, needs, and requirements of the specific project when choosing the development criteria, in order to choose the more suitable ones to the context at hand.

It is clear that this methodology focuses on a socio-technical approach. For the system to be efficient and successful, the technology must be entirely adaptable to the social and organizational factors. Thus, it is evident that the technical features are not seen as the most important aspect in the development of a system. Work satisfaction, and overall satisfaction of the users are the key purposes of the IS development process.

Mumford (1993) states that ETHICS includes the following design tools:

- A framework to support the identification of the goal, main tasks, significant limitations, and other important aspects to an effective development;
- A variance analysis tool to assist the definition of systematic and operational problems;
- A questionnaire to evaluate the level of work satisfaction;
- A framework to define what is expected to change both internally and externally;
- A set of procedures for individual and group work development.

To sum up, the ETHICS method is based on the notion that, in order to be successfully implemented, an information system must efficiently combine both social and technical aspects (Avison and Taylor 1997). It has a distinct philosophy regarding other methodologies used in IS Development, because it is based on organizational behavior and it sees development as fundamentally related to the process of change, not only as a technical issue.

3.2.6 STRADIS Methodology

Structured Analysis, Design and Implementation of Information Systems, also known as STRADIS, was originally developed by Chris Gane and Trish Sarson in 1979. It is a methodology based on structured process modeling, where complex problems are divided in a detailed and formal way. It is a step-by-step methodology which focuses on a structural approach based on data (Litan et al. 2011); thus, it works better in contexts where there is evident need for prioritization, due to the project's size, restrained deadlines, etc.

According to Avison and Fitzgerald (2003), the STRADIS approach was developed in the era that they refer to as the "Early Methodology Era." It is comprised of all methodologies that are centered on the development of computer-based applications through emphasis on planning and step-by-step processes, which is the case with STRADIS. It was considered that such methods would improve the management of systems development and introduce discipline—an approach that has come to be known as the Systems Development Life Cycle (SDLC).

As the name implies, this is primarily a structured methodology. Such models are "based on functional decomposition, that is, the breaking down of a complex problem into manageable units in a disciplined way" (Avison and Fitzgerald 2003). STRADIS focuses on the selection and interassociation of components and interfaces that can decipher a specific problem. The objectives of the project must be clear and well defined from the start, because STRADIS, and similar methods, are

Fig. 3.3 Stages of STRADIS methodology

largely oriented toward problem solving (Litan et al. 2011). On the other hand, it gives much emphasis to the tools and techniques that should be used to solve a given situation, instead of simply providing a detailed description of what constitutes each step in the process (Britts 2011).

Similarly to SSADM, STRADIS is based on a top-down functional analysis method, where the system is divided into subsystems using graphical representations, primarily data flow diagrams (DFDs) (Litan et al. 2011). These will facilitate the creation of an outline and overview of the system that is going to be developed.

STRADIS is essentially comprised of four consecutive stages (Britts 2011), summarized in Fig. 3.3. A careful and well-documented analysis of the problem, as well as existing possibilities and solutions, is the axis that forms this process, hence STRADIS being considered primarily as a problem-solving methodology. Its main purpose is evidently to provide a systemic, disciplined guide to approaching a project.

It can be concluded that this methodology addresses many of the more crucial issues of IS development, such as costs, advantages, benefits, and a detailed examination of the system that is being designed and developed. However, user experience is given a secondary role, as part of the detailed study on the existing system but with no participatory power. This leads to the consideration that STRADIS is much more appropriate for situations where the objectives are clear, but user requirements are uncertain or diffuse (Avison and Taylor 1997).

3.2.7 Information Engineering (IE)

Information engineering methodology (IEM) is an architectural approach that aims at providing a framework for planning, evaluating, developing, and implementing applications within an organization. Its primary goal is to enable an organization to improve the administration of its resources.[1]

IE is "an integrated, full lifecycle systems development approach with automated tool support" (Hogan and Raja 1997), that is particularly useful in introducing

---

[1] Definition available at Lecture notes in information technology http://www.ier-institute.org/2070-1918/lnit25/lnit%20v25/i.pdf.

discipline and rigor on the development process. The idea is that the automation of work tasks facilitates the entire process by leaving room for the analysis and designing aspects of a system's development (Hogan and Raja 1997). It is essentially a data-oriented methodology (Zaied et al. 2003) and its primary tools are enterprise models, data models and process models, worked in a top-down process (Zarvic and Daneva 2006).

This methodology not only focuses on the organizational purposes, but also places great emphasis on the information infrastructure on which to base management of the process, allowing the team to supervise their own project (Aouad et al. 1993). It is seen as a framework outlining a variety of techniques that are used to develop and design IS effectively.

IE is rooted in the idea that different variables involved in a given system are brought together in order to develop a cross-functional system (Hogan and Raja 1997). One popular tool to achieve this is the automated computer-aided software engineering (CASE toolset), essentially a set of programs and automated mechanisms that allow the project to be developed but also monitored and controlled (Hogan and Raja 1997).

IE is structured as a method to collect and effectively apply information from the real world into the desired system. According to Roberts (2010), this translates into a process shaped like an inverted V, where information is acquired by sensors and transported into an operating system which will allow for that data to be processed, and eventually analyzed. After analysis and inference, the operating system is modeled and controlled into an output hardware, and this will impact the real world, through the system's actuators.

IE is a flexible method that can be adapted to specific contexts and projects, but is evidently more focused on the tools and concrete methods of IS development than the less obvious elements such as user satisfaction.

3.2.8 Jackson Systems Development (JSD)

The Jackson systems development (JSD) is a "method for specifying and designing systems whose application domain has a strong temporal flavor and contains objects whose behavior is describable in terms of sequences of events" (Jackson 2002). This IS development methodology appears as an extension of the program design methodology referred to as Jackson structured programming (JSP), a method centered on the premise that programs must process one or more sequential streams of data. The JSP was extended to JSD with the purpose to design and implement information systems (Jackson 1992).

Because JSD derives from JSP, Jackson (2000) states that this methodology was based on the principles of program design. An information system can be seen as a simulation, or model, of the "real world," with further functionality to offer the information outputs. The real world, in this context, is viewed as a collection of entities such as customers, products, or accounts. For that reason, this methodology

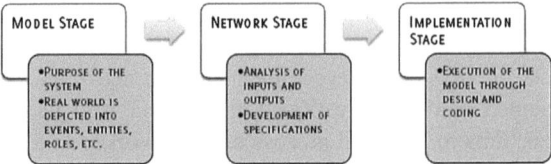

Fig. 3.4 Stages of JSD

can be seen as a new approach to reality-driven methodologies that center on designs associated to reality, and information-driven methodologies that have a propensity to focus on data and processes.

Consequently, the main purpose of JSD is to guarantee that the final system is an accurate reflection of not only the developer's but also the user's perceptions of the real world, by considering the current state of the real world and describing it (Rohde 1995). This methodology, much like soft systems methodology and similar approaches, also attempts to bridge the gap between technical issues and real-world contexts. It is rooted on established criteria for modeling real-world entities, and the conceptual separation of system specification and system implementation (Savage and Mingers 1996).

For Cameron (1986) and Jackson (1992), there are three stages to a JSD methodology, as outlined in Fig. 3.4. The starting point is the premise that the real world is comprised by sequential components ordered in time, called events or actions, and the process will begin by acknowledging which of these components are of interest to the issue at hand. So, the first stage (modeling) is essentially concerned with the real world, not with the system that is being developed. This event list is the first mechanism by which the scope and purpose of the system is defined, followed by an identification of relevant entities and common actions. All of these components are organized into event and data models (Jackson 1992).

The network stage essentially entails the analysis of the processes and connections that flow between the various components of the system, described in the model stage. These connections are organized into a system specification diagram, with different shapes representing different forms of process communication (Jackson 1992). Thus, a systemic description of inputs and outputs of the system is achieved, allowing for the development of the new system's specifications.

Finally, the implementation phase is mainly based on two issues: scheduling of the process specifications, and organization/management of the data. The tools and techniques used in this stage are essentially the tools of JSP (Jackson 1992).

The JSD methodology has been used to develop systems of all sizes. However, the characteristic rigor of this methodology can make it considerably complex to use.

3.2.9 Information Systems Work and Analysis of Changes (ISAC)

Information Systems Work and Analysis of Changes, known as ISAC, was developed in the 1970s at the Institute for Development of Activities in Organizations in Stockholm, Sweden. It is a methodology for IS development that centers on the client's needs, and it was created in order to guarantee that the business gets the IS it requires. Therefore, it starts with thorough analysis of the organization's present situation and the specific problem, and aligns the development of the system by the perspective of that analysis. It maintains the emphasis on the organization's specific issues and needs, by encouraging the participation of users and all other stakeholders in the development process, monitored by the developers (Wieringa 1996).

Nilsson (1989) states that the ISAC methodology, in general, spans two main development areas. Change analysis consists of the examination of problems, and possible solutions, for business activities in a company. ISD consists of the analysis and design of the IS as a support to the business activities.

The ISAC approach is based on the notion that by establishing an IS, one alters the environment, rather than creating a new one (Hanani and Shoval 1986). Moreover, ISAC is a methodology oriented to the problem, which attempts at specifying its root causes and solutions. But because it is focused on business demands, it is essentially used for client-oriented development.

ISAC can be divided into four stages that focus on user and management questions. The following table (Table 3.3) defines each of the four stages, according to Wieringa (1996).

ISAC is primarily focused on problem analysis and activity modeling, while neglecting data modeling techniques, which lead to some researchers combining it with data modeling methodologies of IS development in order to improve its flexibility (Wieringa 1996).

It can also be asserted that ISAC is not adequate for complex control systems (Wieringa 1996). Its encouragement of user participation and preference for meetings rather than documentation means it stands closer to the agile spectrum of IS development and therefore is more suitable for client-focused projects with dynamic requirements.

Table 3.3 Stages of ISAC

Change analysis	The main goal is to identify the organization's needs, by identifying the problem and what changes need to be performed in order to overcome it
Activity study	The selected model of the situation is broken down into information subsystems, so as to allow for the identification of essential features and interfaces between the subsystems
Information analysis	A specification of which inputs and outputs the IS has, and what are the quantitative requirements of each subsystem
Implementation	A decision is made on the technology that will be used to build the IS, and it is designed and programmed accordingly

3.2.10 Multiview Methodology

The multiview methodology was first outlined in 1985 by David Avison and Trevor Wood-Harper, based on their experience with systems analysis in the industrial context (Avison and Wood-Harper 2003). Since then, it has been improved and expanded, eventually becoming an important alternative in the field of IS development (Avison et al. 1998). It was created as a reaction to traditional IS development methods, which had firm roots in engineering discipline and technical rationality (Vidgen 2002).

According to Avison and Wood-Harper (2003), multiview's fundamental principles are centered around five essential questions that any IS development needs to address:

1. How can the system contribute to the organization's goals?
2. How can it be adjusted to the worker's daily routines?
3. What is the most efficient way for the users to interact with the system?
4. What functions will the system need to perform?
5. What technical specifications can more easily achieve the desired results, based on the previous four questions?

Each of these five questions was associated with a different dimension of the framework: in a hierarchical, progressive structure, these dimensions were *human activity, information, socio-technical, human–computer interface,* and *technical.* The structure and its meanings are illustrated in Fig. 3.5.

This five-stage framework shows that the multiview approach allows an adjustment along the process of IS development, by considering not only the technical aspects, but also focusing in the human assets and how their skills and concerns can influence the process. These five stages are considered necessary to develop a system that is complete and balanced in technical as well as human aspects.

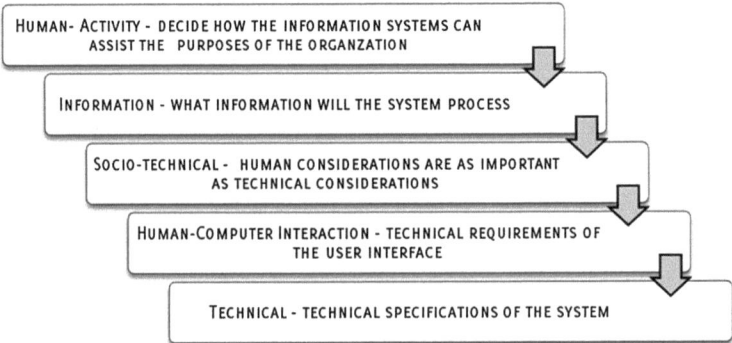

Fig. 3.5 Multiview methodology framework [adapted from Avison and Wood-Harper (2003)]

Furthermore, it can be asserted that this methodology combines five different views that are important for the successful development of a project, by covering all the important features. Avison et al. (1998) state that this framework moves "from the general to the specific, from the conceptual to hard fact, and from issue to task."

Multiview can be considered as an intricate methodology for two key reasons: it combines "hard" and "soft" techniques; and since it is a contingent approach, it does not follow a strict, step-by-step direction (Avison and Wood-Harper 2003).

Since information systems are constantly evolving and changing, the multiview methodology also evolved. The refined version of Multiview is known as Multiview 2. It is an expansion of the Multiview 1, mainly building on the importance of analyzing and studying how an information system must be used and adjusted at the software level (Avison et al. 1998). It attempts to enhance the framework by substituting the waterfall-like scheme of Multiview 1 by a more dynamic model that can better illustrate the relationships between organizational behaviors, work systems, and technical artefacts. Here, the development process is broken down into four stages (organizational analysis, information modeling, socio-technical analysis and design, technical design and construction), with the process of IS development mediating the scheme (Avison and Wood-Harper 2003).

Multiview attempts to address real-world problems. It includes phases, which are related to the human and social dimensions as well as the technical aspects. It attempts to address all questions related to the organization as a whole, such as the people working in the organization, the human–computer interaction, the various purposes that the information system has to carry out and the technical aspects for executing those functions.

3.3 Conclusion

According to Avison and Taylor (1997), ISDMs are commonly categorized according to specific subjects or characteristics. We have discussed a variety of the most popular ISDMs, and following the system presented by Avison and Taylor (1997), the following categories can be inferred:

(a) Process-oriented methodologies that are appropriate to well-structured problem situations and focus on the structure of the system design, presenting structured guidelines;
(b) Methodologies used on unstructured problems, where the purpose is uncertain;
(c) Methodologies that promote elevated user interaction with the system;
(d) Methodologies that combine features from other models.

Based on the above ISDMs categorization, we can classify the presented ISDMs as described in Table 3.4.

These categorizations are not to be seen as an absolute truth. All these methodologies have in common the main purpose of improving and facilitating an information system development process. In addition, several methodologies or

Table 3.4 Categorization of ISDM

Design-oriented	Agile
Structured	SSADM, SSM, JSD, STRADIS
User-oriented	ETHICS, ISAC
Focus on organizational aims	IE
Hybrid	Multiview

situations may fit into more than one category of the presented classifications (Avison and Taylor 1997).

We have presented, in some detail, some of the ISDMs that are used in the context of information technology and information systems. The adaptation of an organization to a new IS should never be unidirectional: the IS should be designed accordingly with the context, the situation, and the end users. This adaptation is facilitated by the adoption of one of the presented methodologies in accordance with the purpose of the IS.

References

Abbas, N., Gravell, A., & Wills, G. (2008). Historical roots of Agile methods: Where did "Agile thinking" come from? In P. Abrahamsson, R. Baskerville, K. Conboy, B. Fitzgerald, L. Morgan, & X. Wang (Eds.), *Agile processes in software engineering and extreme programming* (pp. 94–103). Berlin: Springer.

Abrahamsson, P., Conboy, K., & Wang, X. (2009). "Lots done, more to do": The current state of Agile systems development research. *European Journal of Information Systems, 18*, 281–284.

Adman, P., & Warren, L. (2000). Participatory sociotechnical design of organizations and information systems—An adaptation of ETHICS methodology. *Journal of Information Technology, 15*, 39–51.

Allen, B. (2000). Individual differences and the conundrums of user-centered design: Two experiments. *Journal of the American Society for Information Science, 51*(6), 501–520.

Aouad, G. F., Kirkham, J. A., Brandon, P. S., Brown, F. E., Cooper, G. S., Ford, S. S., et al. (1993). Information modelling in the construction industry: The information engineering approach. *Construction Management & Economics, 11*(5), 384–397.

Ashworth, C. M. (1988). Structured systems analysis and design method (SSADM). *Information and Software Technology, 30*(3), 153–163.

Avison, D., & Taylor, V. (1997). Information systems development methodologies: A classification according to problem situation. *Journal of Information Technology, 12*, 73–81.

Avison, D., Wood-Harper, A., Vidgen, R., & Wood, J. (1998). A further exploration into information systems development: The evolution of Multiview2. *Information Technology & People, 11*(2), 124–139.

Avison, D., & Wood-Harper, T. (2003). Bringing social and organisational issues into information systems development: The story of multiview. In S. Clarke, E. Coakes, M. G. Hunter, & A. Wenn (Eds.), *Socio-technical and human cognition elements of information systems* (pp. 5–21). Hershey: Information Science Publishing.

Avison, D., & Fitzgerald, G. (2003). Where now for development methodologies? *Communications of the ACM, 46*(1), 79–82.

References

Aydin, M., Harmsen, F., Van Slooten, K., & Stegwee, R. (2004). An Agile information systems development method in use. *Turkish Journal of Electronic Engineering, 12*, 127–138.

Britts, W. (2011). *The relationship between organizational and national culture and the use and effectiveness of systems development methodologies* (Master's thesis, North-West University, South Africa). Retrieved from http://dspace.nwu.ac.za/handle/10394/9165.

Cameron, J. R. (1986). An overview of JSD. *IEEE Transactions on Software Engineering, 12*(2), 222–240.

Checkland, P. (2000). Soft systems methodology: A thirty year retrospective. *Systems Research and Behavioral Science, 17*, 11–58.

Conboy, K. (2009). Agility from first principles: Reconstructing the concept of Agility in information systems development. *Information Systems Research, 20*(3), 329–354.

Edwards, H. M., Thompson, J. B., & Smith, P. (1989). Results of survey of use of SSADM in commercial and government sectors in United Kingdom. *Information and Software Technology, 31*(1), 21–28.

Gasson, S. (1995). The role of methodologies in IT-related organizational change. In *Proceedings of BCS Specialist Group on IS Methodologies, 3rd Annual Conference: The Application of Methodologies in Industrial and Business Change*, pp. 1–14.

Goodland, M., & Riha, K. (1999). SSADM—An introduction. Retrieved from http://www.dcs.bbk.ac.uk/~steve/1/index.htm

Gould, J., & Lewis, C. (1985). Designing for usability: Key principles and what designers think. *Communications of the ACM, 28*(3), 300–311.

Gulliksen, J., Göransson, B., Boivie, I., Blomkvist, S., Persson, J., & Cajander, A. (2003). Key principles for user-centred systems design. *Behaviour and Information Technology, 22*(6), 397–409.

Hanani, M., & Shoval, P. (1986). A combined methodology for Information Systems analysis and design based on ISAC and NIAM. *Information Systems, 11*(3), 245–253.

Hardman, J., & Paucar-Caceres, A. (2011). A soft systems methodology (SSM) based framework for evaluating managed learning environments. *Systemic Practice and Action Research, 24*(2), 165–185.

Hevner, A., March, S., Park, J., & Ram, S. (2004). Design science in information systems research. *MIS Quarterly, 28*(1), 75–105.

Highsmith, J. (2002). *Agile software development ecosystems*. Boston: Addison-Wesley.

Hirschheim, R., & Klein, H. K. (1994). Realizing emancipator principles in information-systems development—the case for ETHICS. *MIS Quarterly, 18*(1), 83–109.

Hogan, P., & Raja, M. K. (1997). Information engineering implementation in organizations: A study of factors affecting success. *Journal of Information Technology Management, 8*(3), 33–44.

Jackson, M. (1992). Jackson development methods: JSP and JSD. In J. Marciniak (Ed.), *Wiley encyclopaedia of software engineering* (pp. 585–593). New York: Wiley.

Jackson, M. (2000). The origins of JSP and JSD: A personal recollection. *IEEE Annals of Software Engineering, 22*(2), 61–63, 66.

Jackson, M. (2002). Jackson development methods. In J. Marciniak (Ed.), *Wiley encyclopaedia of software engineering*. New York: Wiley.

Litan, D., Apostu, A., Copcea, L., & Teohari, M. (2011). Technologies for development of the information systems: From ERP to e-government. *International Journal of Applied Mathematics and Informatics, 5*(2), 137–152.

Manteghi, N., & Jahromi, S. (2012). Designing accounting information system using SSADM1 case study: South fars power generation management company (S.F.P.G.M.C.). *Procedia Technology, 1*, 308–312.

Mao, J.-Y., Vredenburgh, K., Smith, P. W., & Carey, T. (2005). The state of user-centered design practice. *Communications of the ACM, 48*(3), 105–109.

Mumford, E. (1993). The ETHICS approach. *Communications of the ACM, 36*(6), 82.

Mumford, E. (2000). A socio-technical approach to systems design. *Requirements Engineering, 5*, 125–133.

Nilsson, A., (1989). Information Systems development: A frame of reference and classifications. In *Proceedings of the First International Conference on Advanced Information Systems Engineering, CAiSE'89*.

Paelke, V., & Nebe, K. (2008). Integrating Agile methods for mixed reality design space exploration. In *Proceedings of the 7th ACM Conference on Designing Interactive Systems, ACM*, pp. 240–249.

Patel, N. V. (1995). Application of Soft systems methodology to the real world process of teaching and learning. *International Journal of Educational Management, 9*(1), 13–23.

Roberts, S. (2010). *Introduction to information engineering*. Retrieved from http://www.robots.ox. ac.uk/~sjrob/ox_teach.html

Rodríguez-Ulloa, R. A., Montbrun, A., & Martínez-Vicente, S. (2011). Soft system dynamics methodology in action: A study of the problem of citizen insecurity in an Argentinean province. *Systemic Practice and Action Research, 24*, 275–323.

Rohde, F. (1995). An ontological evaluation of Jackson's system development model. *Australasian Journal of Information Systems, 2*(2), 77–87.

Sánchez, A., & Mejía, A. (2008). Learning to support learning together: An experience with the Soft systems methodology. *Educational Action Research, 16*(1), 109–124.

Savage, A., & Mingers, J. (1996). A framework for linking soft systems methodology (SSM) and Jackson system development (JSD). *Info Systems Journal, 6*, 109–129.

Schumacher, M. (2001). *The use of SSADM (structured systems analysis and design methodology) as a standard methodology on information systems projects*. Munich: GRIN Publishing GmbH. Retrieved from http://www.grin.com/en/e-book/106034/the-use-of-ssadm-structured-systems-analysis-and-design-methodology-as

Sharma, S., Sarkar, D., & Gupta, D. (2012). Agile processes and methodologies: A conceptual study. *International Journal on Computer Science and Engineering, 4*(5), 892–898.

Tajino, A., James, R., & Kijima, K. (2005). Beyond needs analysis: Soft systems methodology for meaningful collaboration in EAP course design. *Journal of English for Academic Purposes, 4*, 27–42.

Tumbas, P., & Matkovic, P. (2006). Agile vs traditional methodologies in developing information systems. *Managment Information Systems, 1*, 15–24.

Venturi, G., & Troost, J. (2004). Survey on user centred design integration in the industry. *ACM International Conference Proceedings of the Third Nordic Conference on Human-Computer Interaction* (pp. 449–452).

VersionOne (2013). 8th Annual State of Agile development survey. Retrieved from http://stateofagile.versionone.com/

Vidgen, R. (2002). Constructing a web information system development methodology. *Info Systems Journal, 12*, 247–261.

Vredenburg, K., Mao, J., Smith, P., & Carey, T. (2002). A survey of user-centered design practice. In *Proceedings of CHI'2002 Conference on Human Factors in Computing Systems (Amsterdam)* (pp. 471–478).

Wallach, D., & Scholz, S. (2012). User-centered design: Why and how to put users first in software development. In A. Maedche, A. Botzenhardt, & L. Neer (Eds.), *Software for people—Fundamentals, trends and best practices* (pp. 11–38). Berlin: Springer.

Wieringa, R. J. (1996). *Requirements engineering: Frameworks for understanding*. Wiley, New York.

Wong, E., & Tate, G. (1994). A study of user participation in information systems development. *Journal of Information Technology, 9*, 51–60.

References

Zaied, A., Aal, S., & Hassan, M. (2003). Rule-based expert systems for selecting information systems development methodologies. *International Journal of Intelligent Systems and Applications, 9*, 19–26.

Zarvic, N., & Daneva. M. (2006). Challenges and solutions in planning information systems for networked value constellations. In M. Weske & M. Nüttgens (Eds.), *Proceedings of the EMISA 2006 Workshop: Vol. P-95 of LNI - Lecture Notes in Informatics* (pp. 119–131). Hamburg: Gesellschaft für Informatik.

Chapter 4
Web Site Development Methodologies

4.1 Introduction

The progress of the World Wide Web appears to be an inexorable process, constantly presenting new challenges and opportunities. With the need to accompany a society that is increasingly dedicated to new technologies, while at the same time reducing costs and improving information systems, entities must equip themselves with the means to attract more customers and users. Thus, a Web site is no longer seen merely as a means to present informative content. Today, it is also a platform for business, communications, and social interaction. Therefore, it is expected that entities innovate their Web pages, so as not to become outdated and out of touch with their user base, unsuited to its evolving and demanding needs.

With the evolution of the World Wide Web and the increasing need to innovate Web sites, researchers have attempted to propose different methods and techniques to aid and improve the development of Web pages. Many Web developers base their work on existing software development methodologies; however, there are specific aspects of Web development that have lead researchers to propose that specific methodologies are needed. Here, we will discuss some of those methodologies by reviewing existing literature, a method which will allow for a useful perspective on the state of research in this field.

4.2 The W3DT Methodology

The World Wide Web Design Technique, commonly known as W3DT, is a pioneering approach used for the design of Web-based hypermedia applications (Bichler and Nusser 1996). Developed by Bichler and Nusser (1996), it was conceptualized particularly for the development of large Web sites. It is a technique focused on the collaborative development of distributed Web pages, allowing for the modeling of highly structured, database-like information-domains, and conventional hypertext. Thus, it facilitates the process of developing both structured and unstructured Web pages, supporting static and dynamic content alike. It also facilitates the creation of unified Web sites, by utilizing submodels for each location, making it an ideal methodology for large-scale Web sites (Bichler and Nusser 1996).

The W3DT methodology comprises an intuitive graphical model suitable for the use of Web pages, which describes design components such as sites, pages, index, forms, menus, links, dynamic links, etc. (Enguix and Davis 1999).

According to Bichler and Nusser (1996), the process of developing a Web site within this framework is divided into two stages:

First, the developers outline a graphical representation of the Web site and respective pages, which will account not just for the aesthetic presentation of the Web site but also its navigational structure. This is accomplished by building one or more *diagrams*. These diagrams consist of at least one page, with optional links, and a layout, which will define formatting specifications for each page. The underlying structure of each page is composed of three elements: form, index, and menu (Bichler and Nusser 1996). These components are the basic design primitives of the W3DT model, as outlined in Fig. 4.1.

Second, the developers produce and run prototypes using a computer-based environment. This stage utilizes a computer-based design environment that the authors called WebDesigner, giving the developer the opportunity to create a running prototype of the Web site. WebDesigner is W3DT's CASE tool, providing this methodology with an intuitive browser that allows the developers to graphically represent the Web site as it is being developed, and to draw and edit all features of its constructs (Bichler and Nusser 1996).

W3DT combines a modeling technique with a computer-based design environment. It was primarily created to support the requirements of unstructured, hierarchical domains. It is a visual, high-level methodology that harnesses the functionality of HTML, its fundamental language (Burner 2002).

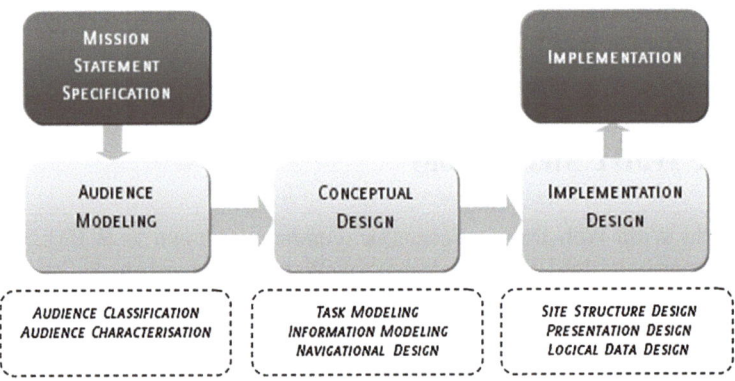

Fig. 4.1 A model of WSDM (adapted from Plessers et al. 2005)

4.3 The Web Site Design Method

The WSDM was first proposed by De Troyer and Leune in 1998. Originally, the acronym WSDM stood for Web Site Design Method, and only concerned Web sites providing information. With the evolution of the World Wide Web, WSDM has developed to encompass not only traditional Web applications but also semantic Web applications, which lead to it being renamed as Web Semantics Design Method (Troyer et al. 2008).

The Web Site Design Method is primarily a user-centered methodology, placing the user at the center of the development of the Web site. It focuses on an audience-driven design philosophy, where the product is design with the audience in mind. Thus, the developer must take into consideration the different potential target audiences (visitors and users). Their necessities and preferences must be the starting point for the design process. This means that the key structure of the Web site is derived from the preferences of the target audience, resulting in different navigation paths (named audience tracks) offered from the home page, one for each different kinds of user/visitor (Troyer et al. 2008).

Its ultimate purpose is to break down multiple design problems by offering a systematic, multiphase approach to Web design. Therefore, each design phase focuses on one specific feature of the Web design cycle, such as requirements and task analysis, data and functionality modeling, navigation modeling, presentation modeling and implementation (Plessers et al. 2005).

WSDM is a methodology which not only offers modeling primitives, allowing Web developers to design and develop models that portray the Web site/application from different perspectives and at different levels of abstraction, but, in addition, it also proposes a systematic way to develop the Web application (Troyer et al. 2008). Since this methodology is not merely attached to a technology, it does not entail the design and structure of the data. Its main concern is to identify potential users and their information necessities (Burner 2002). Thus, it can be asserted that the management of information is at the center of this methodology.

The WSDM comprises five fundamental stages (Troyer and Leune 1998), which are summarized in Fig. 4.1. There is a preliminary stage, the *mission statement specification*, during which the purpose and goals of the Web site are outlined, as well as its subject and target users (Plessers et al. 2005). The second stage is *user modeling*. Here, it is crucial to focus on the potential users of the Web site. This stage is divided into two phases: user classification and user class description, where the users are identified and classified. A user class is a division of the potential users who are equal in terms of their information requirements. The second stage is *conceptual design,* and it is also divided into two steps: object modeling, where the information requirements of each distinct user classes and their perspectives are properly described by developing a conceptual object model for each of the different user classes, and navigational design, where a navigation model is developed. The navigation model presents a navigation track that communicates how users can navigate through the existing information. The third stage is *implementation design*. At this point, the "look" of the Web site is developed. The purpose is to produce a reliable, enjoyable, and efficient "look" for the conceptual design made in prior stages. The fourth stage is *implementation*, the actual completion of the Web site, and its placement online.

When developing an application with this methodology, the developer must follow a well-defined design philosophy that will aid him/her with the necessary support to organize the Web site. With the WSDM, development comprises a chain of successive stages. Each stage has a well-defined output. Therefore, for each stage, a (sub) method that illustrates how to obtain the output from its input is offered. The output of one phase is the input of a following phase (Troyer et al. 2008).

The implementation of WSDM guarantees that autonomic computing elements can be accessed in a regular way and have well-defined life cycles. Furthermore, each of the elements is regarded as a resource that is addressable through the Web Services Addressing Standard (Litoiu et al. 2008).

Burner (2002) argues that "WSDM is good to design front-ends and design the 'look and feel,' but it does not either explicitly design, or manage dynamic data. It is advisable to combine it with a second methodology to design the structure of the data and dynamics."

4.4 Relationship Management Methodology (RMM)

The Relationship Management Methodology (RMM) was originally developed in the 1990s, as a framework for the design and construction of hypermedia applications. It is thus called because it focuses on hypermedia applications as a vehicle for the relationships between information objects (Isakowitz et al. 1995).

RRM is a structured methodology. The design stages of the process are preceded by a number of studies focusing on such things as the objectives of the Web site, market and user analysis, information sources and permissions, distribution channels, and cost–benefit analysis. This results in feasibility studies, as well as a thorough knowledge of both information and navigational requirements (Isakowitz et al. 1995).

After needs, goals, and requirements of the project are well defined, there follows a process of seven stages, as illustrated in Fig. 4.2.

E-R Design The information domain of the application is represented via an Entity–Relationship (E-R) diagram. According to Isakowitz et al. (1995), this first step of the design process represents a study of the relevant entities and relationships of the application domain.

Entity Design This step establishes how the information in the selected entities will be presented to users and how they may access it. The resulting concept is described as an E-R+diagram. It involves dividing an entity into meaningful pieces and organizing these into a hypertext network.

4.4 Relationship Management Methodology (RMM)

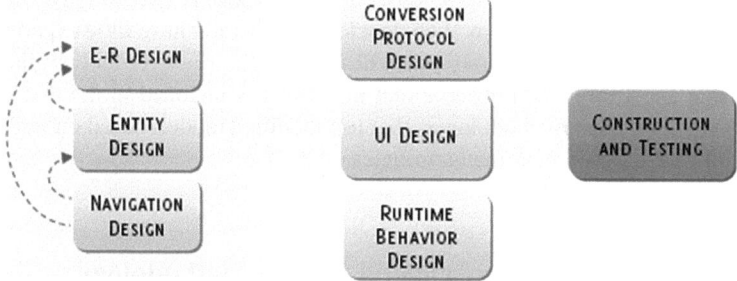

Fig. 4.2 A simplified model of RMM (adapted from Isakowitz et al. 1995)

Navigational Design The course that will enable hypertext navigation is outlined and designed. Each associative relationship appearing in the E-R+ diagram is examined and represented in a Relationship Management (RM) diagram.

Conversion Protocol Design Developers use a group of conversion rules to convert each element of the Relationship Management Data Model (RMDM) diagram into an object in the target platform.

User Interface Design Design of screen layouts for every object appearing in the diagram acquired in Step 3.

Runtime Behavior Design At this point, developers make decisions about which link traversal, history, backtracking, and navigational mechanisms are to be applied. It is important to consider the instability and the dimension of the domain in order to choose whether node contents and link endpoints are to be developed during application, or dynamically computed on demand at runtime.

Construction and Testing This last step consists on the implementation of the application and testing.

Applications designed with this methodology are represented in RMDM, based on the E-R model and the Hypermedia Design Method (HDM), which was one of the first methods created to identify the structure and interaction of hypermedia applications. RMM combines a top-down and a bottom-up approach (Koch 1999). The Data Models thus created allow the breaking apart of the attributes of a given object or entity into *slices*, and the grouping of entities into *m-slices*. The concept of slice is here meant to mediate between the logical architecture of the Web site, and its presentation, as each slice contains the information that will be displayed (Antoniol et al. 2000).

RMM is particularly adequate to the development and implementation of Web sites focusing on relational databases. It allows for the portrayal and development of the application domain in an abstract way, and it describes all elements of the application domain regarding entity types, attributes, and relationships, through the inclusion of the Relationship Data Models (Antoniol et al. 2000). However,

Howcroft and Carroll (2000) have observed that RRM is exceedingly complex, which makes it less adaptable, as Web developers generally have little experience in the IS field, and this methodology relies heavily on IS principles and terminology.

Venable and Lim (2001) observe that the RMM is included in the category of Web site development methodologies that use modified models based on traditional IS or software development methodologies.

4.5 Object-Oriented Hypermedia Design Methodology (OOHDM)

The focus of a hypermedia application is information, and the principle that information can be divided into smaller parts regardless of how it is presented or stored. Schwabe and Rossi (1995a) argue that the Object-oriented Hypermedia Design Method (OOHDM) uses abstraction and composition mechanisms in an object-oriented model, in order to allow for a concise description of complex information items and permit the specification of complex navigation patterns and interface transformations.

OOHDM is essentially based on Hypermedia Design Model (HDM), a method that focuses on the notion of hypertext as the conjunction of entities and their relationships, such as navigational paths. However, OOHDM expands HDM toward the object-oriented paradigm, where design activities permit composition mechanisms (for example, classification, aggregation, and inheritance hierarchies), leading to abstraction and reuse by introducing several visual schemas to improve the expressiveness of the model (Burner 2002). Contrary to HDM, OOHDM presents a clearly defined method for the development of hypermedia applications (Gaedke and Graef 2000).

Under the OOHDM methodology, the hypermedia application is developed in a four-stage process sustaining an incremental or prototype process model. Each stage emphasizes a particular design concern, and an object-oriented model is constructed. Classification, aggregation, and generalization/specialization are used throughout the process to improve abstraction power and reuse opportunities (Schwabe and Rossi 1995a). The four stages are described in Table 4.1.

In the *conceptual design* stage, a conceptual model of the application domain is developed using well-known object-oriented modeling standards. As a result, a class schema is produced, consisting of subsystems, classes, and relationships, with multiple-valued attributes and explicitly indicated directions. The goal, at this point, is to aggregate and summarize the domain semantics in the widest and most neutral form possible, without particular concerns regarding users and tasks (Schwabe et al. 1999).

The second stage is *navigational design*, a description and visualization of the navigational structure of the hypermedia application, based on numerous navigation classes such as nodes, links, indexes, and guided tours. The multivalued attributes

4.5 Object-Oriented Hypermedia Design Methodology (OOHDM)

Table 4.1 The four-stage OOHDM (adapted from Schwabe and Rossi 1995a)

Stages	Products	Mechanisms	Design concerns
Conceptual design	Classes	Classification	Modeling the semantics of the application domain
	Subsystems	Composition	
	Relationships	Generalization	
	Attribute perspectives	Specialization	
Navigational design	Nodes	Mapping between conceptual and navigation objects	Takes user profile and task into consideration
	Links		
	Access structures		Emphasis on cognitive aspects
	Navigational contexts		
	Navigational transformations		
Abstract interface design	Abstract interface –objects	Mapping between navigation and perceptible objects	Modeling perceptible objects
	Responses to external events		Implementing chosen metaphors
	Interface transformations		Describing interface for navigational objects
Implementation	Running application	Those provided by the target environment	Performance completeness

described in the conceptual model are corresponded to different navigation classes. OOHDM posits that navigation objects are the concrete components that give form to conceptual objects. Likewise, links also reflect conceptual relationships. The resulting schema, specifying all navigational classes, defines the navigational domain of the hypermedia application. The actual structure of the navigational design is then developed (Schwabe et al. 1999).

The third stage is *abstract interface design*, where an abstract interface model is developed by identifying perceptible objects (such as a picture, a city map…) and interpreting them in terms of interface classes. Interface classes are described as aggregations of primitive classes (such as text fields and buttons). Because user interface is a fundamental aspect of Web development, it is also an essential stage of the OOHDM process. The abstract interface specification will determine the appearance of navigational objects, which objects will activate navigational actions, the synchronization between multimedia elements and the context and purpose of interface transformations. This is achieved by means of Abstract Data Views, formal models that describe structural as well as interactive aspects of the interface (Schwabe et al. 1999).

The fourth and final stage is *implementation*, and it essentially entails the running of the application. A particular attention is now given to the runtime environment. Schwabe et al. (1999) outlined an appropriate environment named

OOHDM-Web, based on the Lua scripting language and the CGI Lua environment. It introduces templates mixing HTML and calls to functions within the navigational library.

These steps are carried out through a combination of incremental, iterative, and prototyped-based development styles. During each step, a set of object-oriented models describing particular design concerns are built or enriched from previous iterations (Schwabe et al. 1996).

OOHDM takes into consideration the very nature of management information systems (MIS), where different users need to access shared data in a way that is adapted for them. A hypermedia application is developed and built as a set of navigational objects that operate as logical windows on a shared conceptual model. By using the OOHDM model, it is possible to create a plan for a domain of hypermedia applications, using recognized object-oriented concepts such as structure and behavior, and abstraction mechanisms, such as aggregation and generalization/specialization (Schwabe and Rossi 1995b).

Ultimately, the purpose of OOHDM is to aid application designers in the development of single-user hypermedia environments. It is also a methodology oriented toward a perceptive model of hypermedia applications, in which users/visitors navigate through a hypermedia space that was authored beforehand (Schümmer et al. 1999). As a result of this orientation, Schümmer et al. (1999) argue that OOHDM is missing some of the possibilities for the design of editing or authoring functionalities that permit the manipulation of the hypermedia space. Therefore, to minimize the lack of editing and management of the hypermedia environment, these authors present the collaborative OOHDM, aimed at facilitating the design of collaborative hypermedia environments. It introduces an interaction design level to the OOHDM, describing the ways in which users/visitors are able to interact with the hypermedia content and with each other.

4.6 Web Engineering

In 1998, a group of researchers established the grounds for Web Engineering, an attempt at creating a new discipline that could introduce sound principles taken from engineering and management into the disorganized panorama of Web development. It was observed that there was little methodical discipline in Web development and that most applications were developed through an ad hoc, contingency plan. But the increasing importance of Web applications, as a separate entity of information systems, called for a new, organized approach (Murugesan et al. 2001).

Web Engineering brings together practices from traditional software engineering methods, adapting them to the more flexible reality of the Web, and other practices that pertain to the specific nature of Web development in itself. It is defined by its creators as "the establishment and use of sound scientific, engineering, and management principles and disciplined and systematic approaches to the successful development, deployment and maintenance of high quality Web-based systems and applications" (Murugesan et al. 2001).

Many developers of Web applications traditionally focused on process logic and data management before moving on to develop the user interface, a practice that derives from the well-established methodologies for software engineering which dated back to the 1960s. But in Web development, user interface is of the utmost importance, as it provides users with an immediate first impression of the Web site's purpose. This has introduced an aesthetic component that did not previously exist, attributing much greater importance to the design stages, and the designers themselves (Deshpande and Hansen 2001).

This is one of the aspects that pertain to the specific nature of Web development as opposed to traditional software development, but there are other aspects such as: The fact that its document-oriented, containing static or dynamic content; its heavy reliance on appearance and visual creativity; a vast, potentially global, user base, with the corresponding variety in profiles and preferences; shorter time frames for development than with regular software; a greater variety in the background, experience, and skills necessary for Web developers than for traditional software engineers (Murugesan et al. 2001).

Web Engineering is centered on the premise that Web development has 6 different dimensions (Deshpande et al. 2002), as illustrated in Fig. 4.3. The authors argue that most existing Web development techniques do not follow all of these stages, starting the project not with planning and management but at a given later stage (Deshpande et al. 2002).

Web Engineering proposes a multidisciplinary approach to development and determines that all of the following stages of development must be taken into account for a solid, successful Web product (Murugesan et al. 2001):

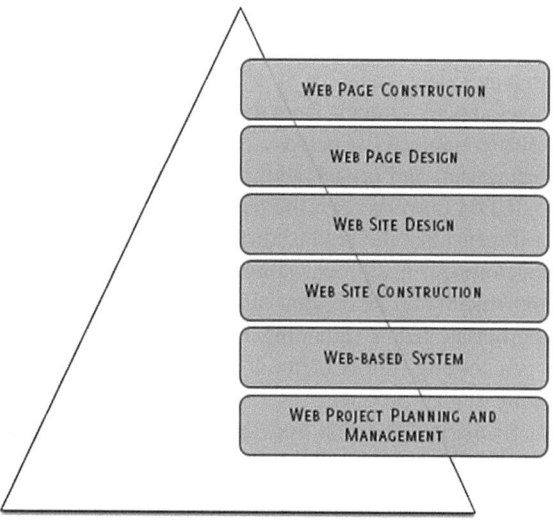

Fig. 4.3 Levels of Web development according to Web Engineering

1. Requirements specification and analysis
2. Web-based system development techniques
3. Integration with legacy systems
4. Migration of legacy systems to Web environments
5. Web-based real-time applications development
6. Testing, verification, and validation
7. Quality assessment, control, and assurance
8. Configuration and project management
9. "Web metrics" for estimation of development efforts
10. Performance specification and evaluation
11. Update and maintenance
12. Development models, teams, and staffing
13. Human and cultural aspects
14. User-centric development, user modeling, user involvement, and feedback
15. End-user application development
16. Education and training

Web Engineering proponents argue that future development models should build on these principles and good practices. Thus, we can assert that Web Engineering is not a methodology per se, but it is a set of standards that is designed to influence or shape future models of development, making it an important milestone in the evolution of Web development methodologies.

4.7 Internet Commerce Development Methodology (ICDM)

As the focus of applications development shifted from traditional information systems to the Web, there was a particular aspect of Web development that captured the attention of researchers: e-commerce. Standing (1999) thus proposed a methodology that would specifically cater to the needs of e-commerce projects within organizational contexts. It was intended as both a management strategy, and a development strategy, heavily focused on business goals and needs. It presents a holistic, subjectivist perspective, aimed at addressing issues of strategic, business, managerial, and organizational culture (Standing 2001).

ICDM proposes that the development of a Web site entails three different levels or dimensions: the organizational level, consisting of a Web management team, the development level, consisting of a Web site component production team, and the implementation level, consisting of all the technical aspects of implementation and appropriate teams (Standing 1999).

According to this methodology, there are seven stages in the process of developing a Web product.

Strategy is the first and the most important: Managers need to determine the organization's competitive situation, by assessing its place in the environment. This is achieved by means of SWOT analysis: an examination of the company's

4.7 Internet Commerce Development Methodology (ICDM)

strengths, weaknesses, opportunities, and threats. The results will depend on the specific conclusions of this process or analysis, which will inevitably vary with the particular conditions of the organization; however, Standing (2001) points out three generic outcomes that determine the scope of the project: "process change" (the modification of a given organizational process using the Internet), "process re-engineering" (complete redesign of a process through use of the Internet), or "transformation" (radical alteration of business practices through use of the Internet) (Standing 2001). This is followed by a substage of *meta-development strategy*, where the Web development team will outline and plan the Web site in relation to business needs, with more or less autonomy, depending on the project and conclusions of the SWOT analysis. Finally, it concludes with a *component strategy*, where the implementation team determines the technical constitution of the Web site's components.

After the strategic aspects of development have been established, there follows an analysis of *logical functional requirements*. This process is heavily user-oriented (Standing 2001). Brainstorming sessions, and similar group communication techniques, are used to provide developers with fast and insightful feedback from all the stakeholders involved, and particularly the intended user base.

With clearly defined strategic principles and requirements, the project can move on to the technical stages of development. *Semi-physical architecture* will establish the framework for the Web site's architecture, defining the combination of document systems, interactive systems, and complex transaction systems that the site will use. *Design* entails all the necessary activities that will provide the Web site with a definitive structure. At this point, it is fundamental to uphold key values of Web design, such as usability, promotion, customer evaluation, and the effective representation of the organization's desired image (Standing 2001).

Implementation and evolution are closely related to the meta-development strategies. Unless the intended Web site is small, it is very likely that not all the content will be established definitively. Some components will remain stable (such as transaction modules), while others will need to evolve continually, a task which should fall under the domain of the Web development team. This team will determine who will have the responsibility of adding and editing the site's content, as well as what guidelines and principles are to be followed in that respect (Standing 2001).

ICDM essentially attempts a multidimensional view in order to bring together the various different perspectives that are formed over the Web-based system (Table 4.2). A combination of different methodologies is, according to the author, the only way to appropriately bridge the gap between these different approaches.

Table 4.2 Different perspectives on Web-based systems (based on Standing 2001)

Focus	Web-based system viewed as
Software application	Programs and logical language
Web site	Design and creation processes
Information architecture	Hardware, network, databases, and software
Specialist application	Application of design and management processes to particular structures (Intranet, extranet)
Business system	A tool for the strategic business goals

4.8 Web Information System Development Methodology (WISDM)

The Web Information System Development Methodology (WISDM) to build Web-based information systems is described in the book "Developing Web Information Systems,"[1] which is authored by Richard Vidgen, Dave Avison, Bob Wood, and Trevor Wood-Harper, and published by Butterworth–Heinemann (2002).

This particular approach stems from the awareness by some researchers that traditional methodologies of system development, such as the System Development Life Cycle (SDLC), the Waterfall methodology or the Rapid Application Development (RAD) model, are inadequate to describe the specific reality and the particular needs of Web development (Shaffi and Al-Obaidy 2013).

According to Vidgen (2002), there are three dimensions that separate system development methodologies from Internet projects. First, in traditional IS development, there is a great deal of abstraction in requirements and strategic principles, while in Web development, the strategic dimension is much more obvious and tangible. Second, in traditional IS development, the typical user is an employee that can be trained and consulted directly, while in Web development, the typical user is essentially a customer who is not required to use the product or train for its usage. Finally, the design of a traditional IS project is focused on pure usability, while on Web development, the product needs to be visually appealing as well as usable (Vidgen 2002).

Therefore, WISDM attempts to provide a framework for connecting traditional systems development methods with Web-based techniques. By using established methods and techniques, it builds on existing best approaches rather than adding a new methodology altogether. It covers the analysis and design activities of an application and/or system development (Vidgen et al. 2002).

In this sense, WISDM builds on the Multiview approach to system development (Vidgen 2002). This is a contigent methodology that is heavily focused on the specific goals of the project and on bridging the gaps between all the different

---

[1] http://www.wisdm.net/wisdm/index.htm.

4.8 Web Information System Development Methodology (WISDM)

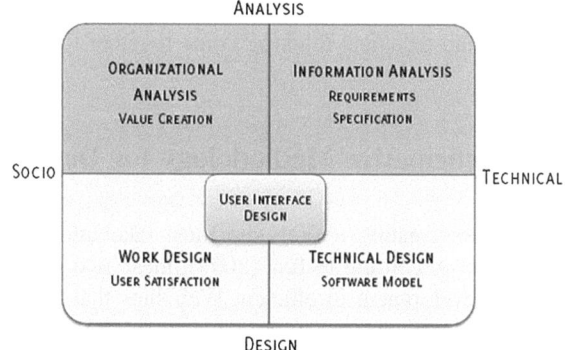

Fig. 4.4 The matrix of WISDM (adapted from Shaffi and Al-Obaidy 2013)

perspectives that different stakeholders will have on the development process. WISDM posits that simple engineering and technical strategies are not sufficient for appropriately building Web applications (Shaffi and Al-Obaidy 2013), which makes the Multiview methodology particularly adequate due to its soft systems approach.

There are five essential aspects that shape the WISDM (Shaffi and Al-Obaidy 2013). These five aspects are reflections of the different levels of influence that will shape the final product, accordingly with its respective stakeholders, as illustrated in Fig. 4.4.

First, the process requires analysis of preexisting conditions. *Organizational analysis* is primarily related to the creation of value in the product. This is the client's goal; the Web site or Web application needs to reflect the organization's business goals, by focusing on market studies and information requirements. *Information analysis* allows the Web developer to further establish and define user requirements, mainly by building documents with graphical notations and/or software prototypes. WISDM commonly uses the UML Model, a representation of the functionality of the system (Shaffi and Al-Obaidy 2013).

After analysis is complete, there follows the design stage. *Work design* is the creation and definition of the relationship between customer and employee, and this essentially entails the principle of designing the site or application with the customer in mind. *Technical design* is the Web site development in itself. It concerns the programming and data structure necessary to create the Web site (Shaffi and Al-Obaidy 2013).

Finally, *human–computer interaction* (HCI) represents the interaction between technical and work design, through user interface (UI) design. UI design is a critical part of the overall Web design development process. This process should combine technical skill, experience, and expectations of the customer/user. The Web developer must focus heavily on the UI design of the Web site, ensuring that it will be effortlessly accessible, usable, flexible, secured, and also supportive of ergonomic features (Shaffi and Al-Obaidy 2013).

WISDM attempts to provide a more encompassing view of the problem of Web development, by proposing a socio-technical view. The Multiview methodology outlines the framework, and WISDM builds on it to propose a construction where creative and technical thinking come together to deliver user-centered content.

4.9 Participative Methodology for Developing Web Sites

Developers creating a Web site must take into consideration usability and HCI principles. According to Issa (2008), these two important aspects are fundamental for the development of efficient Web sites that adequately match basic marketing purposes. Designers and users need to work together within a well-defined methodology to generate a Web site that meets the requirements of the users and creates a need for them to return to the Web site (Issa 2008).

Building on the notion that the designers must consider issues of usability and HCI principles when creating a Web site, Issa (2008) developed a new methodology, named the Participative Methodology for Marketing Web sites, as a result of an intensive study of existing systems development methodologies, marketing methodologies, and other Web development methodologies (Issa 2008). The concept of usability is central to this approach, due to its focus on marketing and sales, which transforms the user into a customer. In the Internet, users have a great deal of information available to them, which allows them to build informed opinions and provides them with variety and choice. If users are faced with a Web site that is difficult to navigate, slow, confusing, and frustrating to use, they will quickly search for a better alternative.

The Participative Methodology proposes a set of stages that the process of Web development should entail. However, these stages are not necessarily sequential, but iterative. The authors have based their model on the Star Life Cycle Model, which places evaluation and testing at the center of the process, as the organizing axis that supports all other activities (Issa 2008) (Fig. 4.5).

The major stages of the Participative Methodology are presented in Fig. 4.5.

Usability Evaluation (SA0) This stage is located at the center of the new methodology, as, before the process moves on to another stage; it is necessary to evaluate the results from the previous stage, which is known as "formative evaluation." *Usability Evaluation—Measurement* (SE0.1): This step is an ongoing evaluation of the Web site to ensure that it achieves its intended purposes.

Functionality Testing (SA1) This stage is also located at the center of the new methodology (along with the usability evaluation) to test the results from the previous stage before moving to another stage. Expert-based and user-based evaluations will test the Web site to ensure that it functions effectively from the technical perspective.

Planning (SA2) This stage allows designers and users to address various project-scoping issues: (1) the requirements for developing a Web site; (2) the nature of the product and the buyers; (3) the firm's competitors; and (4) the location of the site

4.9 Participative Methodology for Developing Web Sites

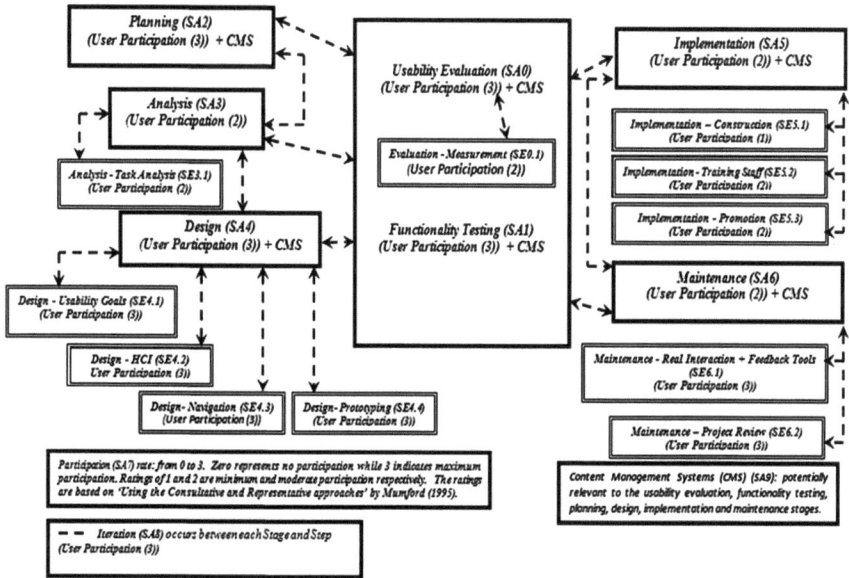

Fig. 4.5 Participative Methodology for marketing Web sites

and how to promote the Web site. In addition, this stage involves developing a detailed schedule of activities required in order to carry out the development of the Web site in an efficient and effective manner.

Analysis (SA3) In this stage, users, analysts, and designers expand their findings in enough detail to indicate exactly what will and will not be built into the Web site design, and to add, improve, and correct the initial Web site requirements if they are not meeting the users' needs and wishes. Analysis—Task Analysis (SE3.1): This step will define the purpose of developing the Web site, the type of users, the type of work users will do with the Web site, users' goals, and their activities.

Design (SA4) The design stage will utilize the requirement specification from the previous stage to define: (1) what the Web site is; (2) how the Web site will work; (3) user involvement in decision-making; (4) future users; and (5) usability requirements. *Design—Usability Goals* (SE4.1): This step will allow users (end users and client–customer users), analysts, and designers (internal and external) to confirm that the Web site design is efficient, effective, safe, useful, easy to learn, easy to remember, easy to use and to evaluate, practical, and visible and that it provides job satisfaction. *Design—HCI* (SE4.2): This step will allow users (end users and client–customer users), analysts, and designers (internal and external) to identify that the Web site design is practical. There are many specific issues that need to be taken into consideration when designing Web site pages, such as text style, fonts, layout, graphics, and color. *Design—Navigation* (SE4.3): This step will define the specific navigation paths through the Web site among the entities to establish the communication between the interface and navigation in the hypermedia application. *Design—Prototyping* (SE4.4): This step is essential in the Web site design process, to allow users and management to interact with a prototype of the new Web site, to suggest changes, and to gain some experience in using it. This step allows the management to reduce costs and increase quality through early testing.

Implementation (SA5) This stage involves the technical implementation of the Web site design. It allows users to use the new product and to check whether it meets their requirements. *Implementation—Construction* (SE5.1): This step involves the technical implementation of the Web site design. *Implementation—Training Staff* (SE5.2): This step will give the necessary training to the staff about the new Web site. *Implementation—Promotion* (SE5.3): This step will use various tools such as press releases, link building and banner-ad campaigns, paid search engines, directory listing campaigns, and traditional marketing methods (e.g., Newspapers, radio, and TV) to promote the Web site.

Maintenance (SA6) This stage involves ongoing maintenance of the Web site, including updating changes and the correction of errors in the Web site. *Maintenance—Real Interaction and Feedback Tools* (SE6.1): During the maintenance stage, real interaction needs to be tracked by using the server log file. This information is very useful to the designers for improving and enhancing the structure and the functionality of the Web site in order to encourage more users to visit it. In addition, feedback tools should be available on the Web site to enable the users to contact the Web site owner for information or personal communication and to provide feedback about the Web site. For example, forms, surveys, discussion forum, contact form, telephone number, and a prize should be available on the Web site to encourage the users to provide feedback about the Web site. The first author recommends that, in order to prevent spam, the organization's e-mail address should not be made available on the Web site. *Maintenance—Project Review* (SE6.2): This step should be available to ensure that the Web site is working toward the project goals. This means that, after putting the Web site online, the designers need to check the Web site after one week to evaluate whether the Web site construction and structure are working according to the users' needs and requirements. One example of a tool that can be used for the project review is a checklist for the goals and objectives, usability, and technical requirements.

User Participation (SA7) This aspect is a very important concept in the methodology, as the main purpose is to allow user participation in the Web site development process in order to gain more information about the problems and alternative solutions from the users and to familiarize them with the system before it is released. For each stage, there is a rating (from 0 to 3), which indicates the extent of user participation in the development process.

Iteration (SA8) This occurs between each stage and step in the Participative Methodology for Marketing Web sites, to check that the Web site does indeed meet users' (end users' and client–customer users') requirements and company objectives before moving to another stage.

Content Management Systems (CMS) (SA9) This aspect is relevant to the usability evaluation, functionality testing, planning, design, implementation, and maintenance stages in the Participative Methodology for Marketing Web sites. This tool will allow the users to manage the Web contents by allowing them to add, edit, remove, and submit information by using various templates and workflows without needing any previous knowledge of the Web site editing tools.

As we have seen, usability and HCI are the principal aspects concerning the development of a Web site through the Participative Methodology. In effect, when usability issues are taken into consideration during the interface development process, various problems can be prevented early on, for example: It can reduce the time needed to access information, it can make the information easily available to users, and therefore, it can prevent the frustration of not finding useful information on the site, which is one of the main reason why users choose not to return to a given Web site. Furthermore, if the Web site is related to electronic commerce and usability principles are not taken into consideration, such problems can directly imply a loss in sales and revenue, which is why this methodology is particularly useful for Web sites in that particular area.

4.10 Conclusion

Contrary to traditional software development, Web site development entails many aspects that are specific to the medium, such as a wide range of possible users, the need to present an attractive image, and a much greater emphasis on usability. Such particular characteristics have led researchers to present methodologies that are thought out specifically for the Web. These methodologies tend to have a more heavy focus on the design processes, more user participation, and a more active maintenance period.

Despite formal differences, all Web methodologies that we have discussed have in common the main purpose of improving and facilitating the Web site design and development process. These methodologies are used with the intention of aiding the Web developers in the process of creating and structuring a Web page. However, it is also paramount that methodologies facilitate the appreciation of information and encourage effective and appealing forms of presentation and provision of information, as a means of promoting products and services. Furthermore, when developing a Web structure, the developers and the organization must guarantee optimum visibility of all the information available in relation to the purpose of the Web site, so as to make sure that the user can access all the information that he/she needs in this one Web site.

References

Antoniol, G., Canfora, G., Casazza, G., & De Lucia, A. (2000). Web Site reengineering using RMM. *Proceedings of the International Workshop on Web Site Evolution* (pp. 9–16).

Bichler, M., & Nusser, S. (1996). Modular design of complex web-applications with W3DT. *Proceedings of the IEEE Fifth Workshop on Enabling Technology: Infrastructure for Collaborative Enterprises (WET ICE '96)*, 328.

Burner, A. (2002). Comparison of web technologies and Web Engineering methodologies. Retrieved June 2, 2014, from http://citeseerx.ist.psu.edu/viewdoc/summary?doi=10.1.1.132.7586.

Deshpande, Y., & Hansen, S. (2001). Web Engineering: Creating a discipline among disciplines. *IEEE Multimedia, 2001*, 82–87.

Deshpande, Y., Murugesan, S., Ginige, A., Hansen, S., Schwabe, D., Gaedke, M., et al. (2002). Web Engineering. *Journal of Web Engineering, 1*(1), 3–17.

Enguix, C., & Davis, J. (1999). Filling the gap: New models for systematic page-based web application development and maintenance. *Proceedings of International Workshop on Web Engineering '99* (pp. 1–9).

Gaedke, M., & Graef, G. (2000). Development and evolution of web-applications using the Webcomposition process model. *Presented at the International Workshop on Web Engineering at the 9th International World-Wide Web Conference (WWW9)*, Amsterdam, The Netherlands.

Howcroft, D., & Carroll, J. (2000) A proposed methodology for Web development. *Proceedings of European Conference on Information Systems* (pp. 290–297).

Isakowitz, T., Stohr, E. A., & Balasubramaninan, P. (1995). RMM: A methodology for structured hypermedia design. *Communications of the ACM, 38*(8), 34–44.

Issa, T. (2008). Development and evaluation of a methodology for developing Websites (Doctoral dissertation, Curtin University of Technology, Australia). Retrieved from http://espace.library.curtin.edu.au/R?func=dbin-jump-full&local_base=gen01-era02&object_id=17908.

Koch, N. (1999). A comparative study of methods for hypermedia development (Technical Report 9901). Munich: Ludwig-Maximilians-University.

Litoiu, M., Mihaescu, M., Solomon, B., & Ionescu, D. (2008). Scalable adaptive web services. *Presented at the ACM ICSE Workshop on Development for Service Oriented Architectures*, Leipzig, Germany.

Murugesan, S., Deshpande, Y., Hansen, S., & Ginige, A. (2001). Web Engineering: A new discipline for development of web-based systems. In S. Murugesan & Y. Deshpande (Eds.), *Web Engineering: Managing Diversity and Complexity of Wen Application Development* (pp. 3–13). Berlin: Springer.

Plessers, P., Casteleyn, S., & Troyer, O. (2005). Semantic Web development with WSDM. *Proceedings of the 5th International Workshop on Knowledge Markup and Semantic Annotation (SemAnnot2005), in conjunction with ISWC 2005* (pp. 1–12).

Schümmer, J., Schuckmann, C., Bibbó, L., & Zapico, J. (1999). Collaborative hypermedia design patterns in OOHDM. *Presented at the HT99 Workshop on Hypermedia Development—Design Patterns in Hypermedia*, Darmstadt, Germany.

Schwabe, D. and Rossi, G. (1995a). The object oriented hypermedia design model. *Communications of the ACM, 38*(8), 45–46.

Schwabe, D. and Rossi, G. (1995b). Building hypermedia applications as navigational views of information models. *Proceedings of the 28th Hawaii International Conference on System Sciences (HICSS '95)* (pp. 231–240).

Schwabe, D., Rossi, G., & Barbosa, S. (1996). Systematic hypermedia application design with OOHDM. *Proceedings of the ACM International Conference Hypertext* (pp. 116–128).

Schwabe, D., Pontes, R. A., & Moura, I. (1999). OOHDM-Web: An environment for implementation of hypermedia applications in the WWW. *SigWEB Newsletter, 8*(2), 18–34.

Shaffi, A., & Al-Obaidy, M. (2013). Analysis and comparative study of traditional and web information systems development methodology (WISDM) towards Web development applications. *International Journal of Emerging Technology and Advanced Engineering, 3*(11), 277–282.

Standing, C. (1999). Managing and developing internet commerce systems with ICDM. *Proceedings of the 10th Australasian Conference on Information Systems* (pp. 850–862).

Standing, C. (2001). Methodologies for developing web applications. *Information and Software Technology, 44*(2002), 151–159.

Troyer, O., & Leune, C. J. (1998). WSDM: A user-centered design methods for Websites. *Proceedings of the 7th International WWW Conference* (pp. 85–94).

Troyer, O., Casteleyn, S., & Plessers, P. (2008). WSDM: Web semantics design method. In G. Rossi, O. Pastor, D. Schwabe, & L. Olsina (Eds.), *Web Engineering: Modelling and Implementing Web Applications* (pp. 303–352). London: Springer.

Venable, J. R., & Lim, F. C. B. (2001). Development activities and methodology usage by Australian web site consultants. *Presented at the 4th Western Australian Workshop on Information Systems Research, WAWISR*.

Vidgen, R. (2002). Constructing a web information system development methodology. *Information Systems Journal, 12*, 247–261.

Vidgen, R., Avison, D., Wood, B., & Wood-Harper, T. (2002). *Developing web information systems*. United Kingdom: Butterworth-Heinemann.

Chapter 5
Usability Evaluation Models

5.1 Introduction

The use of interface and WWW by individual and organizations become an essential to enhance performance and job satisfaction, as these tools should be designed in an efficient way to prevent frustration and vexation among users.

These tools should be friendly, efficient, effective, and easy to use. To ensure if interfaces, systems, and WWW are meeting users' needs, a specific usability evaluation models should be employed before the implementation to examine and assess their functionality and performance, as well as to identify the problems if they are available.

These models will assist designers and HCI experts to generate exceptional solutions to improve users' work and satisfaction and reduce frustration.

Finally, to understand users' mind-sets and performance and to improve the fit between humans and the system, cognitive engineering should be presented.

5.2 Cognitive Engineering

Cognitive involves user activities from thinking, reading, writing, talking, remembering, making decision, planning, solving problems, and understanding people. Norman (1993) discriminates two types of cognitive, namely experiential and reflective. The experiential mode reflects perceive, act and react as it needs a certain level of motivation and enthusiasm, i.e., driving a car, reading a book, playing a video game, or having a conversation. On the other hand, the reflective mode involves thinking, comparing, and decision making. This mode leads to creativity and innovation, i.e., writing a book, designing, and learning. Both modes need specific technologies, as well as are essential for everyday life.

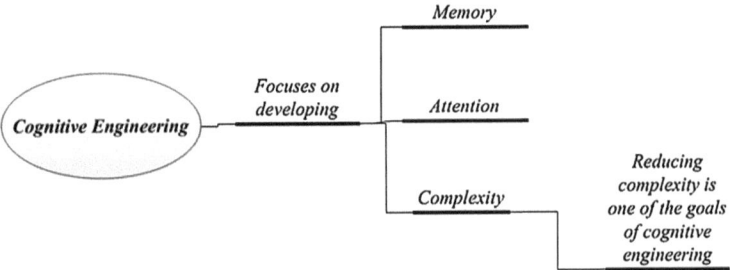

Fig. 5.1 Cognitive engineering—prepared by the authors

Cognitive Engineering focuses on developing systems that support the cognitive processes of users such as memory, perception and recognition, memory, learning, reading, speaking, listening, problem solving, decision making and attention which are used in Human Computer Interaction. The main aim of cognitive engineering is implementing cognitive resources and reducing complication in developing systems (see Fig. 5.1).

To understand the cognitive resources such as memory and attention which are utilized in HCI, there are four types of models, i.e., goals, operators, methods, and selection rules (GOMS); executive process-interactive control (EPIC) model; Adaptive Control of Thought-Rational model (ACT-R); and Adaptive Control of Thought in Information Foraging model (ACT-IF). These models' evaluation aims to assist users to demonstrate and reveal the user interaction with computers and the implications for designers.

5.3 Cognitive Walk-throughs

Cognitive walk-throughs model involves expert users to ensure if the set of activities will meet the correct action of the system. According to Nielson and Mack (1994, p. 6), cognitive walk-thoughts involve "simulating a user's problem solving process at each step in the human-computer dialog, checking to see if the user's goals and memory for actions can be assumed to lead to the next correct action."

An example of cognitive walk-thoughts evaluation is required users to get from one screen to another to obtain a certain tasks done (Preece et al. 2002; Sharp et al. 2011).

There are specific steps involved in cognitive walk-thoughts, based on Preece et al. (2002):

- The characteristics of typical users are identified and documented, and sample tasks are developed that focus on the aspects of the design to be evaluated.
- A designer and one or more expert evaluators come together to do the analysis.

- The evaluators walk through the action sequences for each task, placing it within the context of a typical scenario, and as they do this, they try to answer the following questions:
  - Will the correct action be sufficiently evident to the user?
  - Will the user notice that the correct action is available?
  - Will the user associate and interpret the response from the action correctly?

Finally, as the walk-through is presently complete, a record of critical information is compiled to identify what cause problems and why are recorded.

This involves explaining why users faced these difficulties, notes about side issues and design changes are made, and a summary of the results is compiled. The design is then revised to fix the problems presented. Last but not least, this evaluation records what works and what does not in details, and this will assist the designers to resolve the problems and ensure the system/interface will meet the users' needs at the end.

5.4 Heuristic Evaluation

Heuristic evaluation is called the rules of thumb, as it guide designer and experts to use high-level design principles or heuristics to ensure if the interface elements confirm to the principles and project aims. This evaluation was developed by Nielsen and colleagues (Nielson and Mack 1994), and it was confirmed (Veredenburg et al. 2002) that this evaluation is very cheap, easy to use, and generate effective evaluation without the need for professional evaluators. The evaluation process under this type will evaluate dialog boxes, menus, navigation structure, online help, and so on.

Using this, evaluation requires an acceptance of an incomplete set of heuristics that are simple, easy to understand, and relevant to the product which evaluators can be trained if necessary.

This evaluation consist the following steps, namely: 1) Briefing: defining users' needs and requirements; 2) Evaluation: evaluators to assess and evaluate the interface; 3) Debriefing: to identify the problems and gaps in the interface.

Finally, the debriefing session, under this step, the experts will bring the problems and gaps from the interface, and specific solutions will be generated to meet the new interface needs, and user will evaluate the new interface to ensure if it met their needs or not.

In the evaluation process, heuristic evaluation is essential as users and designers will understand the system/interface functionality well, and this evaluation will define the gaps, and precise solutions will be defined to these gaps in line to match users' needs (Fig. 5.2).

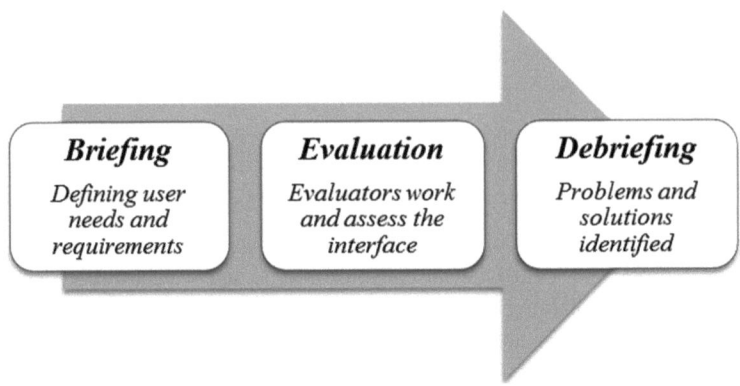

Fig. 5.2 Basic process of heuristic evaluation

5.5 Goals, Operators, Methods, and Selection Rules (GOMS)

GOMS model was developed and invented by Card et al. (1983). This model aims to present the knowledge of determined human computer interaction and how user can interact with computers and the implications for designers. This model endeavors to reduce the complexity in the interface as well as in the cognitive resources and engineering. Under this model, there are specific elements that describe purposeful HCI, illustrated in Table 5.1.

- Goals specify what the user wants and intend to achieve.
- Operators are the building blocks for describing human–computer interaction at the concrete level.
- Methods are sequences of sub-goals and operators to accomplish a goal.
- Selection rules predict which method will be used. For example, "If the mouse is working, select 'point to an item on screen,' if not select choose OPEN option in file menu."

Finally, GOMS model is based on levels of interaction that bridge the gap between the abstract (psychological) task and the concrete (Physical System).

Table 5.1 GOMS

Goals	User needs
Operators	HCI building blocks
Methods	Programs built through operators
Selection rules	Definition of what methods will be used

5.6 Executive Process-Interactive Control (EPIC) Model

EPIC model is a cognitive design for modeling human, multimodal, and multiple-task performance. This model is useful to examine the system or interface speed of processing, working memory capacity, dual-task performance, and other cognitive abilities change by age. This model was developed by Kieras and Meyers for modeling human cognition and performance (Kieras and Meyer 1997; Meyer et al. 2001). EPIC model contains peripheral sensory-motor processors surrounding a production rule cognitive processor and is used to construct précise computational models for a variety of human–computer inaction situations.

EPIC model has several elements, namely (Kidder et al. 1999) modal stores, control store, tag store, and storage capacity.

- The modal stores contain visual, auditory, and tactile stores that contain coded information from modality-specific perceptual processors.
- Control store contains the following:
  - goals (assist to perform particular tasks);
  - steps (assist users to complete their job in a sequence manner);
  - strategy notes (to enable or disable rules for alternative task strategies);
  - status notes (indicate the current state of various processes).
- Tag store includes labels that assign specific roles to modal-store items.
- Storage capacity is focused on task storage and there is no limit of stored items.

Finally, this model is very useful to assess human performance limitations toward the interface/software design from low levels of specific interaction techniques and at high levels of systems that support complex task performance in multimodal time-stressed domains (Kieras and Meyer 1997, p. 394) (Fig. 5.3).

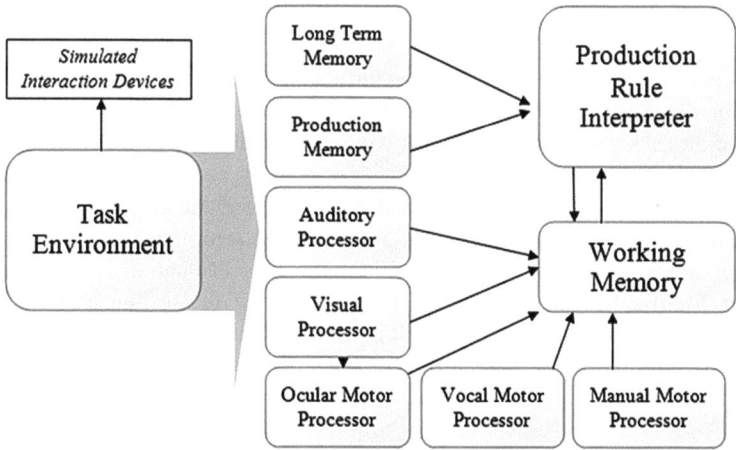

Fig. 5.3 The architecture of EPIC simulation techniques (adapted from Kidder et al. 1999)

5.7 Adaptative Control of Thought-Rational Model

ACT-R is a cognitive design to understand human cognitive psychology and human performance. This model aims to understand how people consolidate knowledge and produce intelligent behavior, as this model will assist users to recall the information from the memory and try to resolve problems by breaking them down into headings and subheadings and later applying knowledge from working memory to generate valuable data. The ACT-R theories are human information processing and knowledge representation theories (Anderson 1993; Hinesley 2007).

There are two types in ACT-R, namely declarative and procedural knowledge. Declarative knowledge involves knowing that something is the case, i.e., Perth is the capital of Western Australia, as well includes various types of knowledge, i.e., goals that are active. However, procedural knowledge involves knowing how to do something, i.e., ride a car. This knowledge involves if/then statements that stipulate how a specific goal can be achieved when specified conditions are met (Whitechill n.d.).

5.8 Adaptative Control of Thought in Information Foraging Model (Act-IF)

ACT-IF model is based on conventional foraging theory metrics and equations that are described by Pirolli and Card (1999). This model presents a cognitive model for information foraging, as the efficiency of information retrieval is calculated by assessments of information scent with heuristic values for the selection of production rules (Spink and Cole 2006; Trepess n.d.). Scent following is the "perception of the value, cost or access path of information sources obtain from proximal cues such as bibliographic citations, WWW, links or icons representing the sources" (Pirolli and Card 1999, p. 646). Pirolli and Card (1999) confirm that if the scent is strong, the information forager can make the correct choice, and if there is no scent, the forager will have to perform a ranking walk-through the environment. Finally, Spink and Cole (2006) confirm that this model aims to examine HCI, information retrieval, and Web systems within information foraging approach based on evolutionary psychology.

In conclusion, this chapter examined and inspected the cognitive engineering and usability evaluation models which are aiming to scrutinize users' reaction and behavior toward interface, WWW and system. This evaluation is a challenging exercise for users, designers and HCI experts, since the testing and evaluation should be presented and performed well in turn to identify the problems well and to enhance the design in sequence to match users' needs.

References

Anderson, J. R. (1993). *Rules of the mind*. New Jersey: Lawrence Erlbaum Associates.

Card, S., Moran, T. P., & Newell, A. (1983). *The psychology of human computer interaction Hillsdale*. NJ: Lawrence Erlbaum Associates.

Hinesley, G. A. (2007). E-learning today: A review of research on hypertext comprehension. *AACE Journal, 15*(3), 255–265.

Kidder, D., Meyer, D., Mueller, S., & Seymour, T. (1999). Insights into working memory from the perspective of the EPIC architecture for modeling skilled perceptual-motor and cognitive human performance. In A. M. P. Shah (Ed.), *Models of working memory: Mechanisms of active maintenance and executive control* (pp. 183–223). New York: Cambridge University Press.

Kieras, D., & Meyer, D. (1997). An overview of the EPIC architecture for cognition and performance with application to human-computer interaction. *Human Computer Interaction, 12*, 391–438.

Meyer, D., Glass, J., Mueller, S., Seymour, T., & Kieras, D. (2001). Executive-process interactive control: A unified computational theory for answering 20 questions (and more) about cognitive ageing. *European Journal of Cognitive Psychology, 13*(1/2), 123–164.

Nielson, J., & Mack, R. L. (1994). *Usability inspection methods*. NY: Wiley.

Norman, D. (1993). Things that make us smart: Addison-Wesley.

Pirolli, P., & Card, S. K. (1999). Information foraging. *Psychological Review, 106*, 643–675.

Jennifer, P., Yvonne, R., & Helen, S. (2002). *Interaction design: beyond human-computer interaction*. New York: Wiley.

Helen, S., Yvonne, R., & Jennifer, P. (2011). *Interaction design—beyond human-computer interaction*. New York: Wiley.

Spink, A., & Cole, C. (2006). Human information behavior: Integrating diverse approaches and information use. *Journal of American Society for Information Science and Technology, 57*(1), 25–35.

Trepess, D. (n.d.). Information foraging theory. Retrieved 1 June 2014, from http://www.interaction-design.org/encyclopedia/information_foraging_theory.html

Veredenburg, K., Mao, J., Smith, P. W., & Carey, T. (2002). A survey of user-centered design practice. In Paper presented at the CHI 02, Proceedings of the SIGHI Conference on Human Factors in Computing Systems.

Whitechill, J. (n.d.). Understanding ACT-R—an outsider's perspective. Retrieved 1 June 2014, from http://mplab.ucsd.edu/~jake/actr.pdf

Chapter 6
Quality Evaluation Models

6.1 Introduction

The 1970s were characterized by a rising demand for technology, and particularly information technology (IT), which started to present a progressively bigger impact on the management and development of organizations and businesses. This increase in demand led to a growing number of problems, particularly when it came to deciding the appropriate information systems (IS) to adopt. The focus then lied on usage and user acceptance: How to predict that the system would be successfully adopted by users? How to make sure it had the appropriate characteristics that users in that organization demanded? It thus became necessary to invest in methods that could help to predict the use of a system to potentiate its success. Researchers started to experiment in this field, which was originating much interest, due to its fundamental importance in the successful adoption of systems inside organizations (Chuttur 2009).

Quality is vital to an interface's success. This is even truer in a competitive milieu where only the systems with high quality prevail (Tian 2004). Hence, quality is an essential requirement for the survival of a system. In order to ensure a system's quality, a multitude of quality evaluation models were developed by researchers, to help determine the system's prospective quality.

The decision of which evaluation models to use must be based on a pertinent and in-depth knowledge of what measures and models are available for system assessment. It is paramount to know their main characteristics prior to their application to a project. The application of these models assists developers in the process of creating systems, so that they can be certain that the system has the necessary quality to be successful and effective. Therefore, the application of an evaluation model has a great impact on the entire development process, allowing for the prediction of key factors of success as well as possible obstacles and how to overcome them. Indeed, the features that these models present include, in many cases, the capacity to detect issues in the system, providing the developers with the opportunity to solve them a priori (Tian 2004).

The field of IS evaluation has been progressing, which is only natural due to the fluid and dynamic nature of IT and IS evolution as a whole. The initial focus on the adoption of IS by users has been extended to comprehend the continuance or discontinuance of IS use (Guinea et al. 2009). Some authors even argue that the stage of development following adoption is more important for the success of IS than the adoption stage itself (Halilovic and Cicic 2013). As this area grew, it became important to assess how the IS were being used after their implementation. The rising interest in understanding what motivates users to continue or discontinue the adoption of IS has given origin to a multiplicity of studies dedicated solely to the exploration of this decision. Many of the models used in the explanation of adoption have also been employed when trying to understand the reasons of users to continue IS use (Guinea et al. 2009). Hence, the evaluation of IS quality necessarily entails the system's adoption but also the continuation or discontinuation of its use.

Aside from having differences in demographic traits, users also have different levels of skills and are culturally diverse. Since evaluation models are focused on the user, it then becomes important to take into account that users come from an assortment of backgrounds and cultures, and this diversity can have a determining effect on their use of technology. "HCI methods and tools are often used cross-culturally before being tested for appropriateness and validity. As new tools emerge, they must be cross-culturally validated to ensure that they work with all audiences, not just those in the country in which they were developed." (Oshlyansky et al. 2007).

All these characteristics were progressively taken into account as researchers and academics developed their models and frameworks for quality evaluation in IS. In the following sections, we will outline and summarize the most significant of these models, thus providing a more panoramic perspective of this growing research field.

6.2 Technology Acceptance Model (TAM)

Developed by Davis (1986) in his MIT Sloan School of Management doctoral thesis, the technology acceptance model (TAM) was one of the first significant attempts to establish a framework for the study of user acceptance and its correlation with quality and system success. It introduced an approach of IS use measurement that accounted for user motivation and the systems' characteristics. According to the author, the idea was to determine the motivational variables that were responsible for the correlation between a system's characteristics and the system's use by end users and, ultimately, to define a way to predict user acceptance when designing and implementing a new system (Davis 1986).

The TAM is fundamentally a description of relationships between the key subjective elements of user acceptance and behavior, and objective (measurable) elements of use and adoption. The core concept is that user motivation is

6.2 Technology Acceptance Model (TAM)

determined by subjective elements such as perceived usefulness and perceived ease of use, which in turn establish the general user's attitude toward using. That attitude will, in turn, determine actual system use. This constitutes a process of ongoing responses that begin when design features are implemented and move from a cognitive response (users' perception) to an affective response (users' corresponding positive or negative attitudes) to a behavioral response (use or discarding of the system). It is noteworthy that "design features" are an external factor here, not having any direct influence over system use, but merely an indirect one, with perceived usefulness and perceived ease of use establishing the causal relationship (Davis 1986) (Fig. 6.1).

The TAM regards the performance of a system in light of two variables: its functionality and its usability. A system's functionality concerns its capacity to act in its specific environment. This analyzes both the systems actions and its consequences in the environment it is applied to. Usability, in its turn, is a fundamental element in the decrease in the financial burden of the resources that are necessary for a system to operate. Also, it implies the need to diminish users' efforts when dealing with the system, and facilitate end users' interaction with the system (Whitworth and Zaic 2003).

TAM is, then, basically supported by two precepts: supposed usefulness and supposed easiness of use. These two precepts are believed to outline the users' behavior of technology adoption. They allow a prediction of how the users will behave toward the adoption of innovative technology (Rao 2007).

In this model, it is evident that the key element is user attitude. Indeed, it is through this stage that systems are, or are not, determined as useful for the purposes of the organization, as well as for individual users' goals. According to Rao (2007), the users' stance with regard to adopting technology is dependent on elements like "perceived ease of adoption, apprehensiveness, perceived utilities of technology (extrinsic motivation); enjoyment (intrinsic motivation)." These factors are determinant in the adoption process because they refer to the users' perspective on that same technology: whether they perceive it as user friendly, whether they have any reserves toward the technology, whether they will find it useful, and whether they will enjoy using such technology. At this point, however, it is important not to

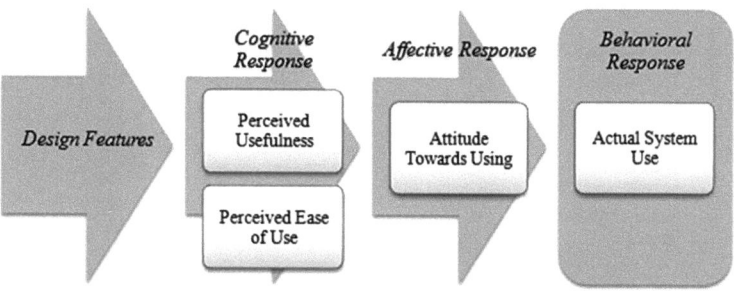

Fig. 6.1 A simple outline of the technology acceptance model (adapted from Davis 1986)

neglect the personal traits of each user, because they will also affect how they will react during the adoption process. Their previous experience with technology, age, social pressure, and qualifications are some of the examples of individual features that may have an impact on how successful the adoption process is (Rao 2007).

In his study of the TAM, Rao has also emphasized the additional component of technology suppliers' commitment, because it is one of the external factors that can condition user attitude regardless of the actual system features. Support provided by the supplier is one example of a component that can determine or influence user perception, even when perceived ease of use is not very positive (Fig. 6.2).

Despite TAM's long existence, the research that has been conducted on this model still has insufficient firmness and pertinence to assure its status as an unmistakably structured theory in the IS arena. Researchers frequently address the TAM, but there is a miscellaneous of viewpoints among them when it comes to TAM's conceptual frame and its value in practice (Chuttur 2009).

The importance of both perceived usefulness and ease of use, in technology adoption, has been well documented in a great variety of empirical studies. Nonetheless, it is the perceived usefulness component of TAM that has asserted its predominance in the field of technology use. The ease of use has been more disputed particularly in the last stages of use, due to its unstable impact. With the continuance of use, individuals begin to feel more confident with the operation and management of the technology, and ease of use becomes less of an impediment (Premkumar and Bhattacherjee 2008). This means that ease of use is a more significant component during early stages of a system's deployment, whereas the system's overall success can be measured in a much longer time frame.

This model, with all its imperfections, was the lead model for IS quality evaluation for almost 20 years, having generated an outstanding number of research studies. Its core power is the fact that it argues that the motivation to use a certain technology has an impact on the behavior of the user and that the motivation of using the technology is intrinsically connected with the perceived usefulness and the perceived ease of use of that technology. At the same time, this belief has also been its major shortcoming. While motivation to use is no doubt a fundamental aspect in quality and success assessment, the focus on this aspect has caused research to neglect other crucial elements of decision making and behavior. "It is

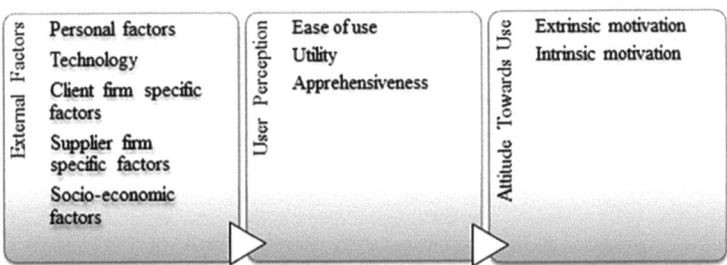

Fig. 6.2 Technology acceptance model in depth (adapted from Rao 2007)

unreasonable to expect that one model and one so simple, would explain decisions and behavior fully across a wide range of technologies, adoption situations, and differences in decision making and decision makers." (Bagozzi 2007).

Nevertheless, the fundamental simplicity of the TAM also makes it very easy to use as the starting point to design a more complex framework. Indeed, many researchers have attempted to expand the TAM, instead of merely creating a new model altogether, which in itself accounts for the usefulness of Davis' groundbreaking work as an outline for research.

6.3 Technology Acceptance Model 2 (TAM2)

The TAM was later expanded upon into what would be designated as TAM 2. This new approach tried to address some of the shortcomings of its predecessor, namely the lack of plausible justifications for a user to deem a system as useful. It was developed by Venkatesh and Davis (2000), who noted that in many of the studies that used the TAM as a research model, the variable of perceived usefulness consistently proved to be the most important variable in determining system use. Therefore, it was necessary to expand that particular concept and pinpoint the determinants of perceived usefulness, and what kind of influence and interactions those determinants could effect on system use (Venkatesh and Davis 2000).

The authors extended the TAM by integrating supplementary theoretical frameworks: *social influence* and *cognitive instruments* (Venkatesh and Davis 2000). By exploring the social influence process and the cognitive instrumental process, TAM2 provides an explanation for the impact of the multiplicity of variables on the two main precepts of TAM: perceived usefulness and behavioral intention (Venkatesh and Bala 2008). Also, TAM2 supports the idea that the perceived usefulness of a technology is influenced by the job's relevance in the sense that if the users possess a full understanding of the knowledge and the tools that concern their work, the adoption of the technology will have a positive effect on job proficiency and hence affect perceived usefulness (Lee et al. 2010).

According to the new interpretation of the TAM, there are three interrelated social forces that can influence an individual who is deciding whether to adopt or reject a system. The first is *subjective norm*, which encompasses the perceived intentions and beliefs of the social web in which the user is inserted, such as the opinions of other people around him/her. The user might not have decided to adopt a system if other people who are considered to be important references to him/her did not endorse it (Venkatesh and Davis 2000).

The second social force is *voluntariness*, understood as *compliance with social influence*, which refers to the degree to which the user perceives he/she has a choice in using the system. It was found, in some studies, that even when users perceive system use to be mandatory, their adoption can vary if they are less willing to adhere to the organizational mandates (Venkatesh and Davis 2000). In this context, it is also important to recognize the role of the internalization of social influence, which refers to the process through which the user integrates the beliefs of the subjective norm into his/her own system of beliefs, thus turning an opinion of others into his/her own opinion. Within an organizational structure, like a company, the role of the "expert power" is an important influence over compliance, as users are more likely to adhere to the opinion of a superior who is considered to have expertise and credibility in regard to the system in question (Venkatesh and Davis 2000).

The third social force involved in influencing perceived usefulness is *image*, as users will often respond to social influence because they want to establish a positive image of themselves. In this context, it is important to pinpoint, during research on IS adoption, whether adoption of the system is perceived as increasing the user's status within the organization, as it will most likely be a factor involved in perceived usefulness of the system. User performance can be a key aspect here, as in many organizational contexts it is one of the primary means of increasing image status (Venkatesh and Davis 2000) (Fig. 6.3).

As we can see, these three processes of social influence are assisted by fundamental key components: *compliance*, which represents the decision to execute a certain action for the purpose of obtaining a reward or avoiding a penalty; *internalization*, which is stands for the individual's adoption of a referent's conviction as his/her own; and *identification*, which means that a person will perform a certain behavior due to his/her belief that by doing so his/her status within a particular group will be improved. It is through these three influential mechanisms that subjective norm and image (the social influence processes) will have a favorable influence over the perception of usefulness (Venkatesh and Bala 2008).

Besides social influence, there are also cognitive instrumental processes. TAM2 distinguishes four factors that, according to research, appear to be more determinant in these processes: job relevance, output quality, result demonstrability, and perceived ease of use (Venkatesh and Davis 2000).

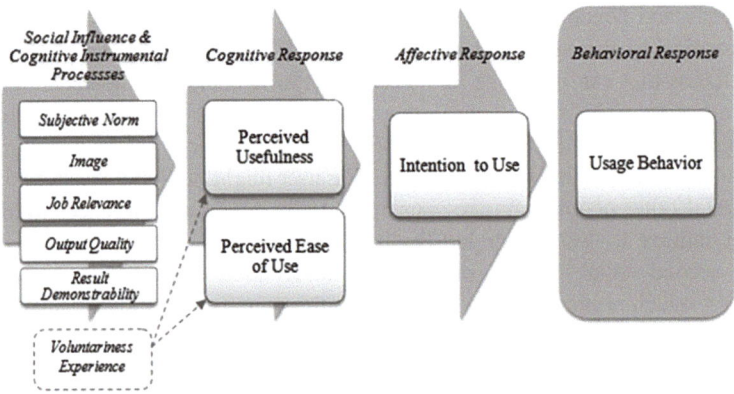

Fig. 6.3 Technology acceptance model 2 (adapted from Venkatesh and Davis 2000)

Job relevance regard the user's perception as to whether or not the system will effectively be applicable to his/her job.

Output quality refers to how well the system performs the tasks that it will be used for, which makes this element conceptually close to that of perceived usefulness; however, output quality is specifically related to a process of measurement where the user, if faced with multiple options, will opt for the one which appears to have the better output quality.

Result demonstrability is the degree to which it is easy to demonstrate the possible positive gains that the system can bring, thus making it more ease for users to have an idea and form a certain perception of its usefulness.

Finally, *perceived ease of use* retains its place from TAM, as "the less effortful a system is to use, the more using it can increase job performance" (Venkatesh and Davis 2000).

Experience is the moderator variable within this model, as experience will affect change within the system's use. The effect of social influence and cognitive processes alike can be substantially impacted as the user gains experience with the system. This is closely related to voluntariness, because if the system's use is mandatory, obstacles to first time use can be overcome, and actual experience with the system will become the predominant criterion. However, not all variables of the model are necessarily affected by experience, and in particular, image and perception of social status gains can persist if the whole organization continues usage, regardless of the user's personal experience with the system (Venkatesh and Davis 2000).

TAM2 allows managers to have a more accurate perception in terms of users' behavior when it comes to technology acceptance. In comparison with TAM, this model has a greater interpretative and descriptive capacity (Javidnia and Nasiri 2012). However, it has been argued that "it omitted attitude to use due to weak predictors of either behavioral intention to use or actual system use" (Tung et al. 2008).

6.4 The Web of System Performance (WOSP)

In 2003, researchers Whitworth and Zaic outlined a new model that attempted a more systemic approach to the issue of IS performance, using general systems theory as a starting point. In this approach, IS performance draws from the same principles and laws of other systems in other fields, such as biology or physics. In fact, it draws from the observation that IS seem to develop and behave much like biological systems, by the laws of evolution. The authors named this model the web of system performance, or WOSP.

The central concept is that of interaction between system and environment, and system performance is defined as "how successfully it interacts with its environment" and if that use continues over an acceptable period of time. Furthermore, there are three aspects that compose the environment and are relevant to determine relationships with the system: the number of opportunities, the number of threats, and the rate at which both change (Whitworth and Zaic 2003).

Interaction between system and environment is determined by four key aspects: "boundary, internal structure, effectors and receptors" (Whitworth and Zaic 2003).

Boundary refers to the need of clearly discriminating between what is the system and what its environment is. The existence of this boundary is the prime aspect of a system's performance, in that it provides the first and most fundamental definition of purpose and goal.

Secondly, it is important to analyze the system's *internal structure*. This consists of assessing the composition of the system, understanding how many parts compose it, and determining what is the dynamics between those various parts.

Finally, *effectors* and *receptors* refer to the different types of feedback between the system and its surroundings. The effectors are the elements that take action in the environment, while the receptors' expertise concerns the collection of information from the environment (Whitworth and Zaic 2003).

These four components are combined with the ultimate purpose of minimizing risk and maximizing opportunity. They are the core of any system's functionality, and in the particular instance of IS, they are at the origin of the eight primordial goals of the system, according to the WOSP methodology (Whitworth 2009) (Fig. 6.4).

In this methodology, WOSP defines eight goals that refer to an IS' ideal traits: "extendibility, security, flexibility, reliability, functionality, usability, connectivity, privacy" (Whitworth et al. 2006). The aims outlined by the WOSP model are characteristics of IS that were already contemplated by researchers, but the innovative factor in this model is the fact that it combines all of them in the same framework. The features are not strange to this field, but their symbiosis into a common structure is original. It is WOSP's multidimensionality that distinguishes it from other models.

This model can be visualized as a web with lines representing the interaction or tension between the different points. Each goal is at a certain distance from the core of the web, and the further it is from the center, the longer is its line, and consequently, the higher is its performance. Hence, the area of the web consists in a

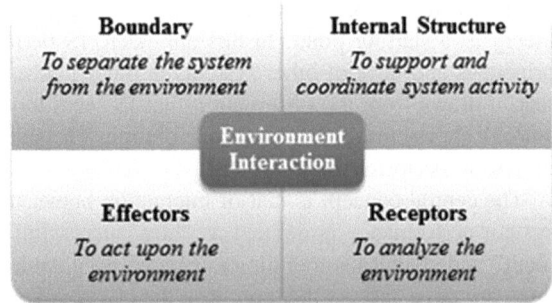

Fig. 6.4 Four aspects of system–environment interaction, according to Whitworth and Zaic (2003)

6.4 The Web of System Performance (WOSP)

multiplicity of lines, illustrating the different levels of performance of all the eight goals.

Each of the eight proposed goals has some relationship to each of the four aspects of system–environment interaction that we have previously described. In that sense, *extendibility* and *security* are the goals of a successful boundary definition, as the purpose is allowing for useful entry into the system as well as protection from harmful entry. *Flexibility* and *reliability* are features that permit the system's internal structure to adapt and survive in the environment. *Functionality* and *usability* will allow for effectors of the system to successfully perform, and *connectivity* and *privacy* are essential aspects for the receptors to manage the analysis of the environment so as to use it in the system's maintenance and development (Whitworth et al. 2006).

The area of the web translates the performance of the system on the whole, so a larger area will mean a potentially more robust system. The shape of the web is a portrait of the system's performance. This shape varies according to the specific features of the system's environment, which might require higher levels of performance from some goals. The shape of the web will highlight those variations. (Whitworth et al. 2006).

Ideally, this web should be balanced. While different systems may determine different shapes, in a general sense, it can be affirmed that a very steep performance increase in one direction of the model may not imply the system's success if it also brings about a very steep decrease in another dimension. So, for example, if a system has very high flexibility but very low reliability, it will most likely not perform well (Whitworth et al. 2006).

It is important to note that in the WOSP model, the concept of performance, where the system's success and quality is determined, is not an absolute concept, but rather it is viewed exclusively in relation to the system's environment (Whitworth et al. 2006). This implies that there is no single definition to determine system performance, because every system will be different when put into context. This fundamentally alters the paradigm set out with the TAM. The TAM was an extremely simplistic model because it aimed at being useful regardless of the system's context, whereas the WOSP model's entire focus is precisely in the possible variations that can occur when context (or environment) is taken into account.

This aspect of the system is demonstrated in Shore and Zhou's (2009) evaluation of the virtual environment Second Life using the WOSP approach. The authors defined each of the goals contemplated by the WOSP model in a manner that would suit the peculiarities of Second Life. All the criteria were used as the model requires, but each of them was assessed and adapted to the specific context of Second Life. This method allowed the authors to reach interesting conclusions regarding numerous aspects of the system, such as Second Life's low flexibility and reliability due to common server lag or downtime, but very high connectivity and extendibility, thanks to an extensive system of user-created content (Shore and Zhou 2009).

The WOSP model thus allowed to pinpoint the strengths and weaknesses of a system in a very specific way. However, the authors also concluded that the precision of this model in terms of mirroring the perception of the users requires more extensive research (Shore and Zhou 2009). Where the TAM focused almost exclusively on the user, the WOSP model's attention to the user is negligible, thus making it relatively unbalanced when studying systems that are very dependent on user interaction, such as social platforms.

6.5 Theory of Reasoned Action (TRA)

The theory of reasoned action (TRA) was pioneered by Martin Fishbein in the late 1960s (Fishbein 1967) and then developed as a joint effort between Fishbein and Ajzen (Fishbein and Ajzen 1975) (Ajzen and Fishbein 1980). It was developed as a framework that enabled the prediction, explanation, and change of individual's social attitudes (Ajzen 2012).

This approach is based on the notion that people's intent to act is rationally affected by their attitudes and that their attitudes are partly determined by their belief system. The TRA presents a method to forecast action, straightforwardness, and ease of maneuver that is based on the assumption that human beings act within reason and rational reactions, and it has been at times classified as one of the most effective attitudinal approaches (Zacharia 2003).

The TRA starts by outlining four different classes of variables that are involved in the process of behavioral actions: beliefs, attitudes, intentions, and behaviors. These variables are all systematically related to one another, and the TRA attempts to provide a framework that describes those interrelationships (Fishbein and Ajzen 1975).

Beliefs are considered to be the fundamental pieces of this model, because they are considered to be the primary source of influence over an individual's attitude, which is described as being the result of a combination of beliefs, and not just a single one. Upon researching the concept even further, the authors reached the conclusion that both individual beliefs regarding a particular behavior and external beliefs (shared in the environment surrounding the individual) constitute the backbone of an intention to perform a behavior (Fishbein and Ajzen 1975) (Fig. 6.5).

Therefore, the starting point in this model is that behavior is directly determined by an intention to perform that behavior (Burak et al. 2013). That intention can be predicted on account of two concepts that, together, provide the outcome of behavioral intent. Those two concepts are as follows: the individual's attitude toward the outcome of the behavior, and the opinions of the person's social environment, here named "subjective norm." Thus, the behavior of a user will depend on whether that user has a positive or a negative understanding of that behavior, and on the subjective norm, which derives from the perceptions that the

Fig. 6.5 Beliefs influence attitudes, which influence intentions, which determine behaviors. Behaviors can create new beliefs

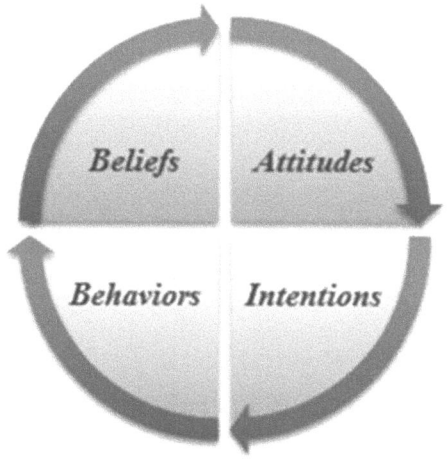

people around the user have in relation to that behavior and the user's drive to act accordingly (Chuttur 2009).

The relationships between beliefs and attitudes, attitudes and intentions, and intentions and behaviors constitute a cycle and not a one-way progress. This is because new beliefs are formed upon performing new behaviors, making the entire process a fluid and ever-evolving one. Changes within the process are arrived at mainly through active participation and persuasive communication, two strategies that expose individuals to information that can have determinant impact on either individual or external beliefs, and ultimately affecting their behavioral choices. The more discrepant that information is in relation to the existing beliefs, the more difficult it will be for it to affect behavior (Fishbein and Ajzen 1975).

TRA argues that individuals can have more than one reference when creating normative beliefs. The usual referents are identified as partners, immediate family, and friends. Nonetheless, in case of specific behaviors, individuals turn to work peers, public authorities, or doctors as referents. The subjective norm is the result of the normative beliefs toward an individual's referents. The subjective norm comes from what a person perceives as being social pressure (Ajzen 2012). The fact that TRA introduced the variable of social influence gave this theory an advantage over other models of technology acceptance and usage (Sun et al. 2013).

Since the TRA has a strong base in user behavior, it is important to underline that one of the most important aspects of external influence over an individual's attitude is cultural context. Hence, some authors argue that the TRA model should account for cultural dissimilarities and be adapted to specific settings. Overview of the body of research suggests that this model is useful for research in developed countries, particularly the USA, but seldom (if at all) used in developing countries or non-Western ones, thus suggesting that greater cultural flexibility is needed (Albarq and Alsughayir 2013).

Fig. 6.6 Model for the theory of reasoned action (adapted from Chuttur 2009)

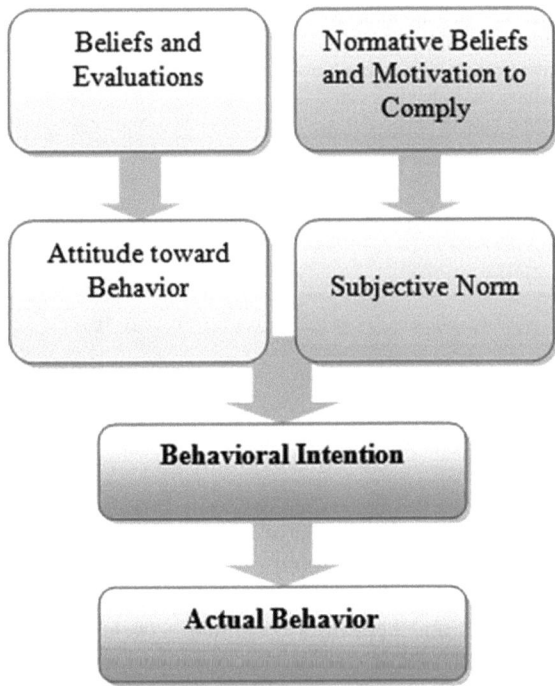

On the other hand, the TRA has been criticized due to its excessively compartmental view on behavior intentions, because of the separation between individual attitude and subjective norm. Some researchers argue that these two variables have an interlinear corelationship between each other and influence each other reciprocally (Burak et al. 2013).

It is important to note that the TRA model, which was designed as a more generic model for the prediction and analysis of human behavioral choices, offered the conceptual starting point for Davis in the development of the TAM, but he made two fundamental changes to the principles of the TRA: The concept of subjective norm was no longer taken into account, because of its vagueness and uncertainty, and the concept of individual attitude toward a given behavior was summarized in two distinct concepts: perceived usefulness and perceived ease of use (Chuttur 2009) (Fig. 6.6).

6.6 Theory of Planned Behavior (TPB)

The theory of planned behavior (TPB) was later presented by Ajzen (1991) as an addition to the TRA model, in an attempt to not only complete it with variables that were previously overlooked, but to also deepen the analysis on the relationships between variables.

6.6 Theory of Planned Behavior (TPB)

While TRA accounts for "attitudinal and normative influence" alone, TPB addresses its shortcomings by taking into consideration the fact that there are behaviors over which people have reduced volitional control, and even when they do have it, they can still pose a great difficulty of execution. Thus, the concept of *perceived behavioral control* was introduced into the original model and taken into account, in order to provide a more realistic approach to the behavior-determining process (Ajzen 2012).

Consequently, the TPB advocates that an individual's actions are driven by "behavioral beliefs about the likely outcomes of the behavior and the evaluations of these outcomes; normative beliefs about the normative expectation of others and the motivation to comply with these expectations; and control beliefs about resources and opportunities possessed (or not possessed) by the individual and also the anticipated obstacles or impediments toward performing the target behavior" (Shumaila et al. 2010).

The introduction of control as a factor represents the most significant difference between TPB and TRA. According to Yzer (2012), perceived behavior control is merely the expression of individuals' understanding of their capacity to perform a certain behavior. It reflects the notion that a user has of his/her own ability to execute the behavior in question. The higher is an individual's perception, the more that individual is expected to act upon that perception, by performing the action in question with resilience. In the same way, the lower that perception is, the less an individual is encouraged to act and the more fragile are his/her attempts to perform the behavior.

TPB also proposes that the attitude that users have toward a specific technology will affect their adoption of that technology. Thus, if people have a positive view in relation to that technology, they will more likely use it, because their positive stance will enhance their motivation of using it. The attitude of the user affects the intention of performing a behavior, and that intention will be determinant in terms of the user's final behavior (Lee 2010) (Fig. 6.7).

Hence, the behavioral intention is originated by the combination of the stance the person has toward that specific behavior, the subjective norm or social pressure, and the perception of control. Generally speaking, people demonstrate a stronger intention to execute a behavior when they have an appreciative opinion about that behavior, which is also shared by their peers, and when they have a high sense of control (Ajzen 2012).

Besides the introduction of control beliefs as the third aspect of intention determination, the TPB also changed the relationships described in the previous model. Behavioral and normative beliefs are codependent; normative and control beliefs are also related because perception of control is first determined within the external, normative context outside the individual; control beliefs directly influence behavioral beliefs, and vice versa, in that the individual's perception of how much control he has over the behavior will influence his belief on the validity of the behavior.

It is also important to note that actual control—regardless of the individual's perception of it—is a part of this model as well, as a completely external factor that,

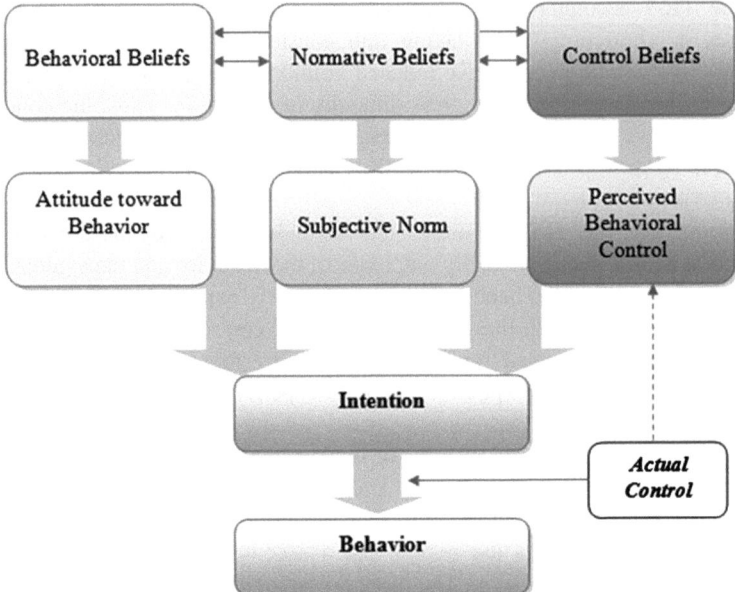

Fig. 6.7 Model for the theory of planned behavior (adapted from Ajzen 2012)

nonetheless, will have a direct influence over the behavior as well as an indirect relationship with the perception of control.

Although the TPB has proved its validity in a great array of research that resorted to its framework as a guideline (Ajzen 2012), there is still criticism to some of its aspects. Perceived behavioral control is a particularly difficult variable to measure and pinpoint with precision, and it is not sufficient to complete the TRA model because there are many other variables that add to the possibility of predicting behavior, such as affective evaluation of behavior (Shumaila et al. 2010). However, this was a reality that was already known upon the development of the TPB, as Ajzen indicated that the model was open to further introduction of new predictors, providing that those new elements had a decisive influence on behavior determination (Ajzen 1991).

6.7 Task–Technology Fit Model (TTF)

The task–technology fit (TTF) model was initially introduced by Goodhue and Thompson (1995), and it is focused on the pertinence of technology in terms of task completion. This model is based on the belief that the adoption of innovative technology is greatly influenced by how it suits the demands of a specific task. The technology is more likely to be adopted the more compatible it is with the particular requirements of a task (Pagani 2006).

In this model, there are three essential components. *Technologies* are tools used in task completion. In IS, this refers to hardware, software and data, as well as user support services. The impact of technology can refer to the impact of a single component (such as an application) but also to the impact of a whole system. *Tasks* are generally understood, in this context, to be the actions that individuals will perform in order to transform an input into an output. In this model, it is more important to focus on tasks that require the user to rely on technologies. Finally, *individuals* are the essential link in the model. Personal traits of the individuals, such as personality or affective emotions as well as training and experience, will determine an effect on his/her use of technology (Goodhue and Thompson 1995).

TTF describes the relation that exists between an individual's decision to adopt a technology and the extent to which the technology is adequate to perform the task that the individual needs to complete. This argument is in line with the concept of perceived usefulness, developed in the TAM. It is based on the same principle: If a system is deemed useful or adequate to perform a certain task, it has a better prospect of being used; thus, it becomes an adequate measure of quality and success. If the gap between the requirements of a given task and the functionalities of the technology used to perform that task becomes too large, TTF is reduced. If the gap is small, and therefore, the technology is adequate, TTF is high (Goodhue and Thompson 1995). However, it is important to note that, unlike the TAM, this model notes that the system's evaluation by users is not just affected by the technology itself, but also by the task, therefore noting that to deem a system as good or bad, it is paramount to determine for what purpose individuals are using that system, and whether it is adequate to that particular objective (Fig. 6.8).

TTF will also have a determining effect over performance impact. Not only is high performance a combination of high efficiency, effectiveness, and quality, but a high TTF will also influence the future perception of the system as useful, which will lead to it being more used in more of the same type of tasks. In this particular aspect, feedback constitutes an important part of the model. User experience will provide other users with positive or negative evaluations, which will affect future expansion of use or the discarding of the system. On the other hand, users can also learn with the system and improve it as they use it, improving the TTF as they do so (Goodhue and Thompson 1995).

Besides establishing a relation between decision to use and usefulness, the TTF model also provides IS developers with guidelines for the design of technology that will potentiate its ideal levels of fitness (Yu and Yu 2010). In that process, there are eight essential characteristics that the technology or system should aspire to: data quality, data locatability, authorization to access data, compatibility between systems, ease of use and training, production timeliness, systems reliability, and relationship with users (Goodhue and Thompson 1995).

The TTF model is closely related to the concept of user performance. The performance of the user when employing a certain technology is greatly influenced by how well that technology fits the task the user needs to complete. Hence, the

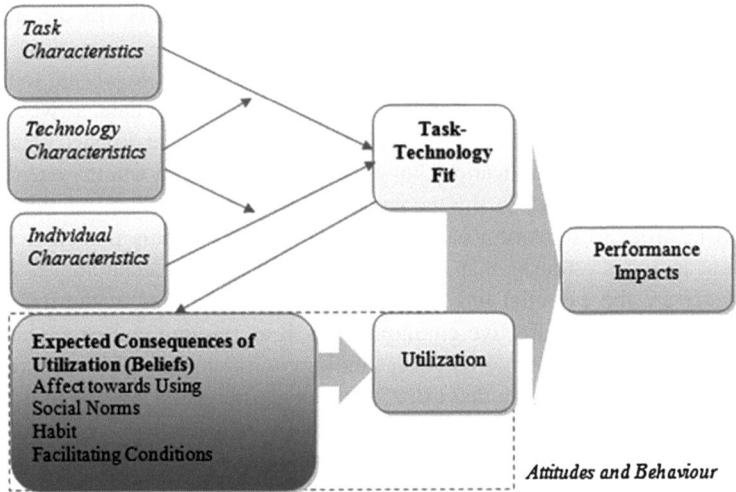

Fig. 6.8 Task–technology fit conceptual model (adapted from Goodhue and Thompson 1995)

more the technology is compatible with the task, the better the user will perform (Chen 2013). This is a crucial aspect because users want to have a good performance, so they will decide for what helps them achieve this objective. The TTF model focuses on the significance of investing in the adequacy of the technology's features in meeting the demands of users; therefore, it is underlined by the notion that individuals' needs should be addressed as a priority in the development and introduction of new technology (Yu and Yu 2010).

The TTF approach is a valuable instrument when the objective is to explore the adoption and the behavior of users of a groundbreaking IT device in a particular setting (D'Ambra et al. 2013). However, some authors have highlighted that TTF neglects the impact of the behavior of the user in terms of technology use and proficiency (Hsin Chang 2010). The approach taken by TTF assumes that users will make a decision in relation to technology depending on its benefits, namely the increase in their performance at work. This approach argues that the user will decide to use the technology that will bring more advantages, independently of their viewpoint toward that same technology (Lin and Huang 2008). But there are many other components to the decision of adopting a technology or system. In fact, Goodhue and Thompson themselves have noted that it was not easy to definitively prove a causal link between TTF and utilization and that an expansion of the model, as well as extensive testing on a greater variety of settings, was needed to improve its usefulness as a research methodology (Goodhue and Thompson 1995).

In accordance with this observation, researchers have attempted to use the TTF framework in combination with other models and theories. Lin and Huang (2008), for example, combined TTF with social cognitive theory (SCT) in a study conducted on knowledge management systems (KMS). This allowed for SCT to add the important behavioral element that TTF lacks, which has been the most often criticized aspect of the model.

6.8 Innovation Diffusion Theory (IDT)

The innovation diffusion theory (IDT) has its origin in the social–psychological research area, and it was designed to explain the practices of adoption, to explore prediction mechanisms and to help with the anticipation of whether a new technology will be successful, and in what way. Originally outlined by Rogers and Shoemaker (1971), it was continually revised in later editions of his work, and its use to explain IT adoption patterns is widely documented in several studies (Wang et al. 2012).

The IDT is conceptualized primarily as a process, designated the *innovation–decision process*, which consists of a set of five consecutive stages of user experience. *Knowledge* is the stage at which the user is first exposed to the innovation and learns how it works. *Persuasion* is the second stage, when the user forms an opinion and attitude toward the innovation. *Decision* happens when the user takes actions that lead to either the adoption or rejection of the innovation. *Implementation* occurs when the user effectively puts the innovation to use. Finally, *confirmation* is the stage at which the user looks for a reinforcement of his/her decision; at this stage, it is also possible to reverse that decision (Rogers 1983) (Fig. 6.9).

This process is initiated on the basis of prior conditions that involve a combination of needs, perceptions, and past experiences of the user, with the social system and environmental context in which the user is active. However, it is not clear whether the need for innovation precedes the knowledge of the innovation, or vice versa, since it is possible that the user never realized he needed that innovation until he learned about it (Rogers 1983).

What is crucial to the IDT is that once users contact with new technology that can benefit them directly, they will obtain, as well as disseminate, information on that technology that will shape their (and others') decision to adopt it or reject it. In this particular stage of the process, the IDT emphasizes the importance of early knowers, those who first gain knowledge of the innovation, as research suggests that people who are involved in early adoption are more self-confident and tend to be more positive than later adopters (Jackson et al. 2013).

Another aspect that is essential to understand the IDT is the role of communication channels in disseminating the information about the innovation along all the stages of the decision process. Communication channels can be constituted by either the mass media or interpersonal exchange. At the first stage of the process (knowledge), the mass media tend to play a bigger role, but interpersonal communication is fundamental at the later stages (Rogers 1983).

IDT is fundamentally based on the premise that new technology is adopted and accepted through the reduction of incertitude. When faced with an innovative technology, people try to obtain information about it and organize what they have

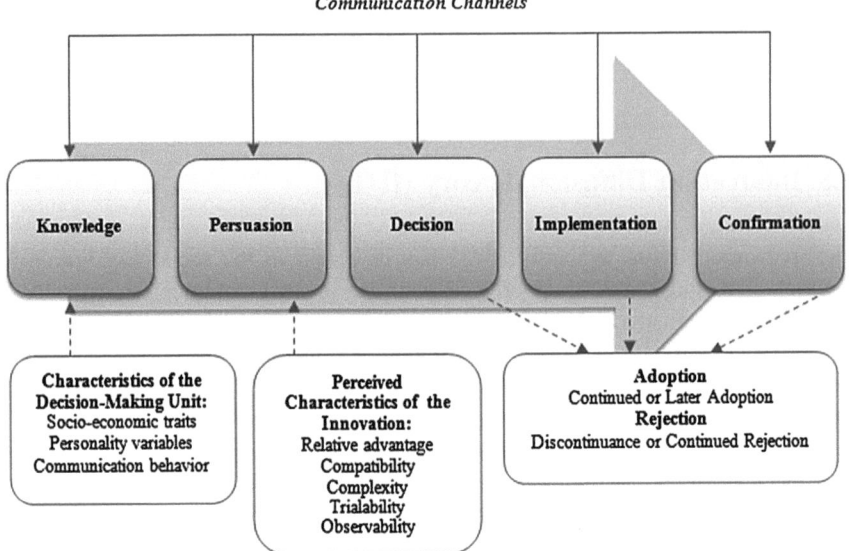

Fig. 6.9 The innovation–decision process (adapted from Rogers 1983)

uncovered. The outcome of this process of collecting information, in order to increase users' confidence in the innovation they have to adopt, is what will determine the users' approval or dismissal of that innovative technology (Nor et al. 2010).

According to the IDT, there are five attributes that innovations can have that will determine user perception and adoption: relative advantage, compatibility, complexity, trialability, and observability (Rogers 1983). Each of these elements has its own importance and contributes to the users' opinion about an innovative technology. However, some studies have concluded that only three of these elements can be unequivocally measured and linked to innovation adoption: relative advantage, complexity, and compatibility (Tung et al. 2008).

The first of these traits, *relative advantage*, concerns the level of perceived benefits that the new technology presents in relation to its antecessor. This notion is comparable to the concept of performance expectancy. *Complexity* refers to the degree of intricacy that the usage of the system will imply. It is in the same line as the traditional definition of effort expectancy. Finally, *compatibility* is the measure of adequacy that a specific technology possesses in relation to user values, work practices, and beliefs (Bhattacherjee et al. 2012).

Besides innovation characteristics, the IDT model also accounts for leader characteristics, particularly those that account for a leader's stance in relation to change. Equally important are the *internal* features of the organization, such as complexity, formality, size and organizational structure, as well as its *external* features, like system openness (Sila 2013).

IDT-based models have been considerably successful in research, particularly in the prediction of social response regarding specific products. The ability to predict the social stance that a product will generate has often sparked the interest of the research community in this framework (Yu and Wang 2007) (Fig. 6.9).

It has also been noted by some researchers that IDT is very complementary to the TAM and both can be combined into a single framework. The most common conclusion in this regard is that compatibility directly influences perceived usefulness and behavioral intention to use, the two key aspects of the TAM (Tung et al. 2008).

6.9 Expectation–Disconfirmation Theory (EDT)

The expectation–disconfirmation theory (EDT), also described as expectation–confirmation theory (ECT), is associated with changes in users' behavior. Originally developed in the fields of marketing and consumer behavior research, it emerged as a methodology to explain the reasons why users' actions change throughout time, and how that change is processed.

The main argument in the expectation–disconfirmation model (EDM) is that user satisfaction is originated by their assessment of the divergence between the expectations they had for a particular service or product before they acquired it, and the opinion they have on its quality after it has been purchased (Wang and Chang 2013). Disconfirmation is determined at the moment the user has contact and experience with the product or service. The theory asserts that satisfaction is correlated with the direction of the disconfirmation, as users will be satisfied if there is positive disconfirmation (the product was better than expected), and they will be dissatisfied if there is negative disconfirmation (the product was worse than expected) (Venkatesh and Goyal 2010) (Fig. 6.10).

We can observe that in the EDT there are three fundamental variables at play: *expectations*, which consist of the beliefs the user has regarding use of the product prior to actually using it; *performance*, which is the user's perception of how the product performed and whether it achieved its goals; and *disconfirmation*, which is a subjective comparison that the user will make after using the product, between how it performed and how he/she expected it to perform in stage 1 (Lankton and McKnight 2012).

IS researchers have adopted the basics of this conceptual model to assert user satisfaction with IT or IS (Bhattacherjee 2001), focusing on the threefold principle that users will first form expectations about usage, which will combine with performance in a second stage, and influence the outcome (decision to continue or not continue usage) in the third stage.

This model is thus able to distinguish the attitude of the user in the preusage and post-usage periods. Users' expectations are the opinions they have about a certain technology prior to its adoption, consisting in the user's viewpoint of the possibilities of that technology's performance, inferred by some of its traits. The performance

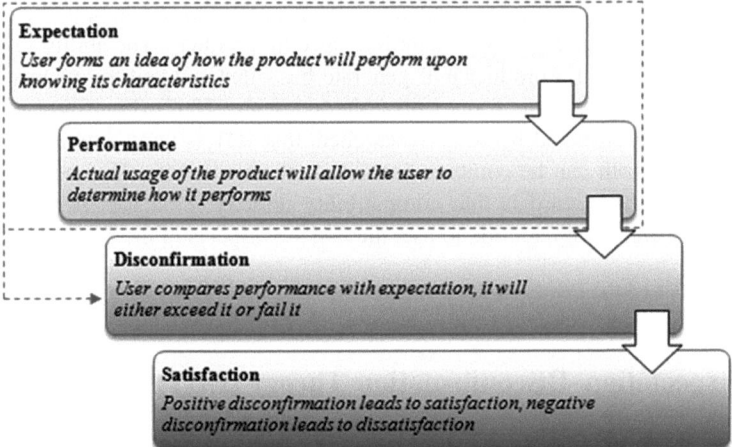

Fig. 6.10 Expectation–disconfirmation model

itself is only measured after the adoption period, when the user confronts the initial opinion with the real performance of the system. When this comparison happens, that is when disconfirmation takes place (Lankton and McKnight 2012). The user realizes that the product or system has inferior quality to that which he/she had expected prior to the purchase or use. Disconfirmation is, thus, a result of users' expectations and his/her perception of quality (Wang and Chang 2013).

This means that the fact that users may initially present a positive attitude toward a system does not necessarily mean that their opinion about the system will remain unaltered. The impact that a change of judgment has on productivity is an important driving force behind the need to understand the process that leads a user to accept a technology or system, at first, and then, with use, to dispute it (Venkatesh and Goyal 2010).

Some authors have noted that expectations can be shaped by more than just the external observation of the technology or system's traits. They may be dependent also on the user's social and cultural context, and on his predisposition to trust the technology or system. Lankton and McKnight (2006) built on this premise to assert that the concept of expectation is linked with the concept of trust in technology. They defined it as "technology trusting expectations," and argued that it appeared to have various dimensions, which they summarized in five sets of characteristics: functionality, reliability, helpfulness, usefulness, and ease of use (Lankton and McKnight 2006). These are the traits that users will base their expectations on.

This model has demonstrated a good performance in the anticipation and understanding of customer satisfaction (Wang and Chang 2013). Hence, it has been applied to studies that investigate a multiplicity of subjects, ranging from a wide scope of areas. The common characteristic between these studies is the fact that they all required a comparison between individuals' perception of the quality of a system/service/product and their expectations toward that same system/service/

product. The EDM is a valuable resource to employ when this comparison has a central impact on decision making (Hsieh et al. 2010).

However, the flexibility and complexity of IS may prevent users from having an expectation of performance for given IS prior to using them. In the situations where the users have no expectations in terms of system performance or cannot acknowledge the type of information IS can potentially provide, the EDM falls short of an explanation for user satisfaction (Au et al. 2008).

6.10 Expectation–Confirmation Model of IS Continuance

Bhattacherjee (2001) outlined a new framework for the EDT, on the premise that previous research wrongfully considered continuance of use as merely an extension of acceptance. Previous models were, therefore, excessively focused on the initial process of technology acceptance and implementation and failed to offer a plausible explanation as to why users can discontinue IS use even though they initially accepted it. Furthermore, there was no consideration for user's motivations after the implementation stage. It was therefore necessary to outline a model that, while drawing from previous research, could focus more on continuance of use (Bhattacherjee 2001).

According to the new ECM, user's motivation to continue to use a certain technology derives from the user's degree of satisfaction with that technology, the level of the user's confirmation of his/her primary expectations, and the opinion the user has in the post-usage period, which appears in the shape of perceived usefulness (Lee 2010).

From this starting point, it is possible to pinpoint a set of premises that were expanded upon through empirical research using this new model.

The first premise is that user satisfaction in the initial employment of a system will have a favorable impact on their decision to continue to use that same system. It is assumed that users become satisfied with IS usage when they confirm their initial expectations about the system. By confirming their primary perception of the system's usefulness, users raise their level of satisfaction (Bhattacherjee 2001).

The second premise is that confirmation plays an important part in the formation of perceived usefulness. Even in situations where the user believed the system to have a limited usefulness, after the experience of using that system, that notion might change into a stronger belief of the system's usefulness. Consequently, the confirmation process has a positive effect on IS perceived usefulness (Bhattacherjee 2001).

The third premise determines that perceived usefulness will have a positive impact on user satisfaction with the system. This had been posited in previous research but usually in relation to the acceptance stage. Bhattacherjee argues that it is also a relevant process during post-acceptance, in continuance contexts. Users will continually rely on a system that they perceive is contributing to high performance (Bhattacherjee 2001).

Thus, the fourth premise is that the intention to continue using an IS derives from perceived usefulness of IS use. It is important to note that while users might have an initial perception of low usefulness, that perception can be adjusted during the confirmation stage, if users realize that their initial expectations were unrealistic. They will *adjust* their perception of usefulness (Bhattacherjee 2001).

In a study developed by Halilovic and Cicic (2013), the authors assessed the level of influence that supporting conditions could have on the intention of continuing to use IS. The ECM was extended to incorporate conditions of support as a determinant element of IS usage continuance. The conclusions of the empirical validation of the extension of this model demonstrated that, by including the element of supporting conditions, the extended model gained a more accurate prediction rate, than the traditional ECM. The results allowed for a new premise to be established: Users' belief in a supporting structure had a significant impact on their perception of the system's usefulness (Halilovic and Cicic 2013).

As with other models, the ECM has been adopted by researchers using other theories or models. This happens when the model is able to explain certain parts of the process of usage continuance, but is insufficient to understand the entirety of the steps that lead to IS continuance. Kim (2010) investigated the continuance of mobile data service, by allying the TPB with the ECM. The author argued that despite the fact that the ECM of IS continuance was a thorough model for the calculation of the core elements behind continuance intention, it neglected the effect of social norm and perceived behavior control. To understand the impact that these two aspects had on IS continuance of use remained an intricate task, which justifies the choice of combining the TPB and the ECM (Kim 2010).

6.11 The Social Influence Model

Vannoy and Palvia (2010) argued that in the literature regarding technology adoption there was not sufficient research on adoption in a broader context, at the level of society, community, or lifestyle. Specifically, they argued that the prevalent models of technology adoption were not appropriate for the study of social computing, which made it urgent to define a model that had that ability, considering the growing role of social technologies in the present day. They suggested that certain constructs of social computing were determinant for this purpose and had direct impact over perceptions of usefulness and ease of use, making the process of technology adoption a twofold construct based on adoption by individuals and embedment in society (Vannoy and Palvia 2010). They named their framework the social influence model (SIM).

SIM is essentially based on the premise that a person will adopt a certain technology or product when there is a considerable amount of people in his/her group that have done so (Young 2009). Therefore, it regards social influence as the element that precedes the adoption of a certain technology. Although the TRA already accounts for a social component of technology adoption, in the concept of

6.11 The Social Influence Model

subjective norm, where the beliefs and the expectations of others play a core part in the decision of the user, it is argued that this term is unfit for the use of technology in current days. This happens because technology has been deeply incorporated in the day-to-day routines of people. SIM aims at being more descriptive of these newer forms of technology, and particularly social technology, because of its significance today.

The concept of social influence as understood by the SIM is outlined by four constructs that the authors have synthesized from the previous literature. These concepts are social computing action, social computing consensus, social computing cooperation, and social computing authority. Social influence is formed where these constructs overlap with each other (Vannoy and Palvia 2010).

The SIM has a very different conceptual foundation than other models which see utility has a major determinant in behavior. In this case, it is not the person's perceived usefulness of a behavior that will affect his/her action; rather, it is *exposure* that will be significant in decision making (Young 2009). In that sense, SIM is in line with the precept that individual action does not follow a rational plan or process, but rather occurs due to the influence of social forces and the interrelationships between those forces (Vannoy and Palvia 2010). In this aspect, it is fundamentally different from the models we have previously discussed, which tend to emphasize the rational process.

The four constructs outlined above, which constitute the variable of social influence, will affect technology adoption in two particular ways: embracement, which is the degree of adoption by the individual (his/her perception of its value and usefulness), and embedment, which is the degree of adoption in the individual's social environment (how many people are using the same technology for the same purposes).

Social influence can therefore be defined as "the degree to which the individual perceives that important others believe he or she should join the group, the degree to which the individual values being a member of the group, the degree to which group membership is perceived important, the degree to which the individual believes in group authority, and the degree to which the individual believes the needs of the group are more important than of the individual" (Vannoy and Palvia 2010).

Social influence in this context appears to also display the three dimensions that the TAM2 describes as social influence processes: compliance, identification, and internalization. Compliance is more adequate for the adoption phase of technology, while identification and internalization are factors that have more potential to predict behavior even after that initial stage (Wang et al. 2013).

It is also important to note that social influence can be transmitted verbally and/or nonverbally. The research in this area focuses mainly on verbal communication, leaving less room for the exploration of the effect of nonverbal interaction. Nonetheless, nonverbal means have peculiar repercussions on individual behavior in the sense that people can reproduce their peer's behavior (Wang et al. 2013).

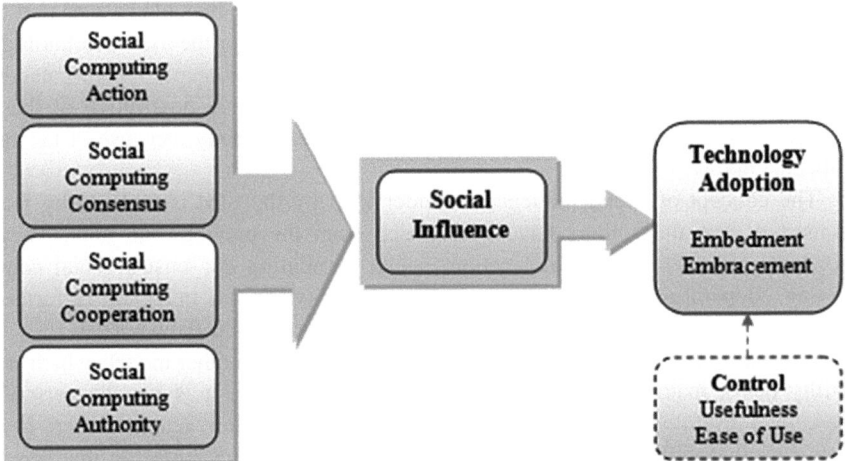

Fig. 6.11 Social influence model (adapted from Vannoy and Palvia 2010)

Since users are now increasingly involved in the development of technology, practitioners need to be aware of this rising engagement with all processes of technology creation and adapt the models they use to assess technology adoption. Furthermore, the impact that social computing is having on conventional business models represents a change in product development that needs to be carefully monitored and addressed in order to respond to the needs and trends of people's usage of technology (Vannoy and Palvia 2010).

The SIM has been often elected as the primordial model when the behavior comes from a group or it happens collectively. This model widened the scope of social influence on behavior intention, which was initially limited to other models' notion of subjective norm, which equaled social pressure (Cheung and Lee 2010). However, one of the shortcomings of the SIM is the fact that other than arguing that people will act according to their peers, this model does not offer a well-defined, broad justification for people's adoption of a product or system (Young 2009) (Fig. 6.11).

6.12 Unified Theory of Acceptance and Use of Technology (UTAUT)

Venkatesh et al. (2003) proposed an entirely new approach to the evaluation of technology usage, essentially combining elements of various research frameworks: TRA, TAM, motivational model, TPB, combined TAM-TPB, model of PC utilization, IDT, and SCT. The new model was named the unified theory of acceptance and use of technology (UTAUT), and it was empirically validated with six

6.12 Unified Theory of Acceptance and Use of Technology (UTAUT)

longitudinal field studies, of six different departments from six large firms in six different areas of industry. The goal was to arrive at a definitive model for IS use that synthesized general knowledge in this field (Anderson and Schwager 2003).

The authors first concluded that, in general terms, there is a common basic premise to user acceptance models, which is as follows: Individual *reactions* to using IT lead to *intentions* to use IT, which leads to actual IT *use*. Use in turn will influence other individual reactions, and so forth. All the models that were used to arrive at UTAUT identify intention and/or usage as the key dependent variable, and UTAUT aimed at understanding this variable in a comprehensive way (Venkatesh et al. 2003).

From this premise, the authors then attempted to arrive at a commonality of variables and factors that act upon intention to use. They arrived at four essential factors: performance expectancy, effort expectancy, social influence, and facilitating conditions (Venkatesh et al. 2003) (Fig. 6.12).

In the context of this model, *performance expectancy* relates to the users' belief in the IS capacity to help them achieve an enhanced job performance. It is regarded as an influential factor in user behavior, since the more individuals expect a system to be helpful in the execution of their job, the more likely they are to use that IS. The concept of performance expectancy encompasses all other similar aspects that were used in previous models: perceived usefulness, extrinsic motivation, job fit, relative advantage, and outcome expectations (Venkatesh et al. 2003).

The second variable of this model, *effort expectancy*, concerns people's conviction of the system's ease of use. Individuals expecting a user-friendly system are more prone to use it. In previous models, this variable was designated as perceived ease of use, complexity, or ease of use (Venkatesh et al. 2003).

Social influence can be defined as the degree to which the user perceives that others around him think he should use the system. A positive feedback from others on his/her use of the system will influence him/her toward using it (Wang and Wang 2010). Previous models used the concepts of subjective norm, social factors,

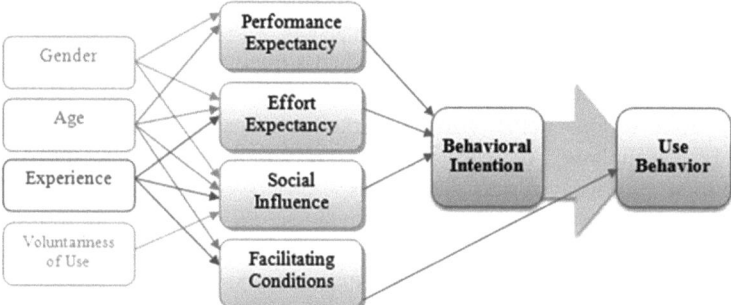

Fig. 6.12 Unified theory of acceptance and use of technology, adapted from Venkatesh et al. (2003)

and image, all three of which can be traced back to this one variable (Venkatesh et al. 2003).

Facilitating conditions refers to the perception a user has of the existence of supporting structures, both at the organizational and technical levels (Sun et al. 2013). The more the user feels that his/her use of the system is supported by the adequate structures, the more likely he/she will use that system. Used in previous models, the concepts of perceived behavioral control and compatibility could fall under this variable (Venkatesh et al. 2003).

UTAUT also establishes four key moderating factors that, while external, will have some degree of influence on the acceptance process: These are demographic factors (age, gender) along with user experience and voluntariness of use (Wang and Shih 2009). These moderating factors can have complex relationships of influence over the rest of the model, but generally, they are more relevant in the initial process of technology adoption (Venkatesh et al. 2003).

The UTAUT model aims to provide a wider depiction of the process of technology acceptance. In their empirical application of it, the authors concluded that "UTAUT explains as much as 70 % of the variance in intention" (Venkatesh et al. 2003). It is an integrated framework that combines the more significant variables presented by previous models, and thus developed a more universal method to forecast and justify users' behavior in terms of technology adoption. Even though it is somewhat recent, it has already motivated several empirical studies by other authors, which have attested for its efficacy (Alawadhi and Morris 2008). It has also presented useful results when applied in contexts other than English-speaking countries, which means that it appears to be solid enough to be used cross-culturally (Oshlyansky et al. 2007).

6.13 Conclusion

As IT and IS became more and more prominent in modern organizational management and technological development, researchers have consistently attempted to pinpoint exactly what causes one system or technology to be adopted by the general user base, and another to be completely rejected. This has been the simplest and most effective way of ascertaining the product's quality.

We have seen that researchers have built numerous models for this purpose, drawing from various fields such as marketing research, social psychology, or behavioral psychology. All these models were tested in empirical studies; some showed more promising results than others.

We can, however, find some commonalities. First, all the most prominent models attribute key importance to individual perception of the technology, regardless of whether this perception is affected by his/her own beliefs or by the social environment.

Second, there is a prevalent notion that individuals will tend to adopt technology on the basis of their perception of its usefulness. Whether "usefulness" means that it is the most appropriate for the task at hand, or the most likely to increase social status or facilitate social interaction, the basic principle is almost always that perceived usefulness constitutes a core component of the adoption process.

And third, the process of actual adoption is moderated by a great number of possible variables of influence, described as subjective norm, social influence, cognitive processes, expectations, etc. All these factors can be traced to the underlying concept that all models share: that the process by which individual perception and beliefs are formed is a complex one. Nevertheless, positive results from empirical studies show that it is possible to predict variation with a sufficient degree to make it useful. Therefore, research on this field will most likely continue to grow, through the evolution, fusion, and/or adaptation of the existing models.

References

Ajzen, I. (1991). The theory of planned behavior. *Organizational Behavior and Human Decision Processes, 50*(2), 179–211.
Ajzen, I. (2012). Martin Fishbein's legacy: The reasoned action approach. *The Annals of the American Academy of Political and Social Science, 640*(1), 11–27.
Ajzen, I., & Fishbein, M. (1980). *Understanding attitudes and predicting social behaviour.* Englewood Cliffs, NJ: Prentice-Hall.
Alawadhi, S., & Morris, A. (2008). *The use of the UTAUT model in the adoption of e-government services in Kuwait.* Paper presented at the Hawaii International Conference on System Sciences, Proceedings of the 41st Annual, Waikoloa, HI.
Albarq, A., & Alsughayir, A. (2013). Examining theory of reasoned action in internet banking using SEM among Saudi consumers. *International Journal of Marketing Practices—IJMP, 1*(1), 16–30.
Anderson, J., & Schwager, P. (2003). SME adoption of wireless LAN technology: Applying the UTAUT model. *Proceedings of the 7th Annual Conference of the Southern Association for Information Systems*, pp. 39–43.
Au, N., Ngai, W., & Cheng, T. (2008). Extending the understanding of end user information systems satisfaction formation: An equitable needs fulfillment model approach. *MIS Quarterly, 32*(1), 43–66.
Bagozzi, R. P. (2007). The legacy of the technology acceptance model and a proposal for a paradigm shift. *Journal of the association for information systems, 8*(4), 3.
Bhattacherjee, A. (2001). Understanding information systems continuance: An expectation-confirmation model. *MIS Quarterly, 25*(3), 351–370.
Bhattacherjee, A., Limayem, M., & Cheung, C. M. (2012). User switching of information technology: A theoretical synthesis and empirical test. *Information & Management, 49*(7), 327–333.
Burak, L. J., Rosenthal, M., & Richardson, K. (2013). Examining attitudes, beliefs, and intentions regarding the use of exercise as punishment in physical education and sport: an application of the theory of reasoned action. *Journal of Applied Social Psychology, 43*, 1436–1445.
Chen, C.-J. (2013). *Using task-technology fit model evaluates trainees' learning performance in Second Life.* Paper presented at the International Conference on Information, Business and Education Technology (ICIBIT 2013), Beijing, China.
Cheung, C. M., & Lee, M. K. (2010). A theoretical model of intentional social action in online social networks. *Decision Support Systems, 49*(1), 24–30.

Chuttur, M. (2009). Overview of the technology acceptance model: Origins, developments and future directions. *Sprouts: Working Papers on Information Systems, 9*(37).

D'Ambra, J., Wilson, C. S., & Akter, S. (2013). Application of the task-technology fit model to structure and evaluate the adoption of e-books by academics. *Journal of the American Society for Information Science and Technology, 64*(1), 48–64.

Davis, F. D. Jr (1986). A technology acceptance model for empirically testing new end-user information systems: Theory and results (Doctoral dissertation). Retrieved from http://web.ffos.hr/oziz/tam/DavisIVenkatesh/Davis_1985_DOKTORAT.pdf

Fishbein, M. (1967). Attitude and the prediction of behavior. In M. Fishbein (Ed.), *Readings in attitude theory and measurement* (pp. 477–492). New York: Wiley.

Fishbein, M., & Ajzen, I. (1975). *Belief, attitude, intention and behavior: An introduction to theory and research*. Reading, MA: Addison-Wesley.

Goodhue, D. L., & Thompson, R. L. (1995). Task-technology fit and individual performance. *MIS Quarterly, 19*(2), 213–236.

Guinea, D., Ortiz, A., & Markus, M. L. (2009). Why break the habit of a lifetime? Rethinking the roles of intention, habit, and emotion in continuing information technology use. *MIS Quarterly, 33*(3), 433–444.

Halilovic, S., & Cicic, M. (2013). Antecedents of information systems user behaviour–extended expectation-confirmation model. *Behaviour & Information Technology, 32*(4), 359–370.

Hsieh, C.-C., Kuo, P.-L., Yang, S.-C., & Lin, S.-H. (2010). Assessing blog-user satisfaction using the expectation and disconfirmation approach. *Computers in Human Behavior, 26*(6), 1434–1444.

Hsin Chang, H. (2010). Task-technology fit and user acceptance of online auction. *International Journal of Human-Computer Studies, 68*(1), 69–89.

Jackson, J. D., Yi, M. Y., & Park, J. S. (2013). An empirical test of three mediation models for the relationship between personal innovativeness and user acceptance of technology. *Information & Management, 50*(4), 154–161.

Javidnia, M., & Nasiri, S. (2012). Identifying factors affecting acceptance of new technology in the industry using hybrid model of UTAUT and FUZZY DEMATEL. *Management Science Letters, 2*(7), 2392–2393.

Kim, B. (2010). An empirical investigation of mobile data service continuance: Incorporating the theory of planned behavior into the expectation–confirmation model. *Expert Systems with Applications, 37*(10), 7033–7039.

Lankton, N. K., & McKnight, H. D. (2006). *Using expectation disconfirmation theory to predict technology trust and usage continuance intentions*. Invited paper presented at University of Minnesota.

Lankton, N. K., & McKnight, H. D. (2012). Examining two expectation disconfirmation theory models: assimilation and asymmetry effects. *Journal of the Association for Information Systems, 13*(2), 88–115.

Lee, M.-C. (2010). Explaining and predicting users' continuance intention toward e-learning: An extension of the expectation–confirmation model. *Computers & Education, 54*(2), 506–516.

Lee, Y.-C., Li, M.-L., Yen, T.-M., & Huang, T.-H. (2010). Analysis of adopting an integrated decision making trial and evaluation laboratory on a technology acceptance model. *Expert Systems with Applications, 37*(2), 1745–1754.

Lin, T.-C., & Huang, C.-C. (2008). Understanding knowledge management system usage antecedents: An integration of social cognitive theory and task technology fit. *Information & Management, 45*(6), 410–417.

Nor, K., Pearson, J. M., & Ahmad, A. (2010). Adoption of internet banking: Theory of the diffusion of innovation. *International Journal of Management Studies, 17*(1), 69–85.

Oshlyansky, L., Cairns, P., & Thimbleby, H. (2007). Validating the Unified Theory of Acceptance and Use of Technology (UTAUT) tool cross-culturally. *Proceedings of the 21st British HCI Group Annual Conference on People and Computers: HCI… but not as we know it*, Vol. 2.

Pagani, M. (2006). Determinants of adoption of high speed data services in the business market: Evidence for a combined technology acceptance model with task technology fit model. *Information & Management, 43*(7), 847–860.

Premkumar, G., & Bhattacherjee, A. (2008). Explaining information technology usage: A test of competing models. *Omega, 36*(1), 64–75.

Rao, A. (2007). *Technology acceptance model for complex technologies in a period of rapid catching-up.* Retrieved October 17, 2007, from http://papers.ssrn.com/sol3/papers.cfm?abstract_id=1016012

Rogers, E. (1983). Diffusion of innovations. In V. Hoffmann (Ed.), *Knowledge and innovation management. Module reader* (pp. 37–50). Hohenheim University.

Rogers, E. M., & Shoemaker, F. F. (1971). *Communication of innovations: A cross-cultural approach*. New York: The Free Press.

Shore, M., & Zhou, Q. (2009). Second life: the future of social networking? *Informal Proceedings of International Conference on Computer-Mediated Social Networking*, pp. 18–27.

Shumaila, Y. Y., Gordon, R. F., & John, G. P. (2010). Explaining internet banking behavior: Theory of reasoned action, theory of planned behavior, or technology acceptance model? *Journal of Applied Social Psychology, 40*, 1172–1202.

Sila, I. (2013). Factors affecting the adoption of B2B e-commerce technologies. *Electronic Commerce Research, 13*(2), 199–236.

Sun, Y., Wang, N., Guo, X., & Peng, Z. (2013). Understanding the acceptance of mobile health services: A comparison and integration of alternative models. *Journal of Electronic Commerce Research, 14*(2), 183–200.

Tian, J. (2004). Quality-evaluation models and measurements. *IEEE Software*, 84–91. doi:10.1109/MS.2004.1293078

Tung, F.-C., Chang, S.-C., & Chou, C.-M. (2008). An extension of trust and TAM model with IDT in the adoption of the electronic logistics information system in HIS in the medical industry. *International Journal of Medical Informatics, 77*(5), 324–335.

Vannoy, S. A., & Palvia, P. (2010). The social influence model of technology adoption. *Communications of the ACM, 53*(6), 149–153.

Venkatesh, V., & Bala, H. (2008). Technology acceptance model 3 and a research agenda on interventions. *Decision Sciences, 39*(2), 273–315.

Venkatesh, V., & Davis, F. D. (2000). A theoretical extension of the technology acceptance model: four longitudinal field studies. *Management Science, 46*(2), 186–204.

Venkatesh, V., & Goyal, S. (2010). Expectation disconfirmation and technology adoption: Polynomial modeling and response surface analysis. *MIS Quarterly, 34*(2), 281.

Venkatesh, V., Morris, M., Davis, G., & Davis, F. (2003). User acceptance of information technology: Toward a unified view. *MIS Quarterly, 27*(3), 425–478.

Wang, H.-Y., & Wang, S.-H. (2010). User acceptance of mobile internet based on the unified theory of acceptance and use of technology: investigating the determinants and gender differences. *Social Behavior and Personality: An International Journal, 38*(3), 415–426.

Wang, W.-T., & Chang, W.-H. (2013). *The integration of the expectancy disconfirmation and symbolic consumption theories: A case of virtual product consumption.* Paper presented at the 46th Hawaii International Conference on System Sciences (HICSS).

Wang, Y.-S., & Shih, Y.-W. (2009). Why do people use information kiosks? A validation of the unified theory of acceptance and use of technology. *Government Information Quarterly, 26*(1), 158–165.

Wang, Y.-S., Wu, S.-C., Lin, H.-H., Wang, Y.-M., & He, T.-R. (2012). Determinants of user adoption of web "Automatic Teller Machines": an integrated model of 'Transaction Cost Theory' and 'Innovation Diffusion Theory'. *The Service Industries Journal, 32*(9), 1505–1525.

Wang, Y., Meister, D. B., & Gray, P. H. (2013). Social influence and knowledge management systems use: Evidence from panel data. *MIS Quarterly, 37*(1), 299–313.

Whitworth, B. (2009). The social requirements of technical systems. In B. Whitworth (Ed.), *Handbook of research on socio-technical design and social networking systems* (pp. 3–22). Hershey, PA: IGI Global.

Whitworth, B., Fjermestad, J., & Mahinda, E. (2006). The web of system performance. *Communications of the ACM, 49*(5), 92–99.

Whitworth, B., & Zaic, M. (2003). the WOSP model: Balanced information system design and evaluation. *Communications of the Association for Information Systems, 12*, 258–282.

Young, H. P. (2009). Innovation diffusion in heterogeneous populations: Contagion, social influence, and social learning. *The American Economic Review, 99*(5), 1899–1924.

Yu, T. K., & Yu, T. Y. (2010). Modelling the factors that affect individuals' utilisation of online learning systems: An empirical study combining the task technology fit model with the theory of planned behaviour. *British Journal of Educational Technology, 41*(6), 1003–1017.

Yu, Y., & Wang, W. (2007). Stability of innovation diffusion model with nonlinear acceptance. *Acta Mathematica Scientia, 27*(3), 645–655.

Yzer, M. (2012). Perceived behavioral control in reasoned action theory: A dual-aspect interpretation. *The Annals of the American Academy of Political and Social Science, 640*(1), 101–117.

Zacharia, Z. (2003). *Using the Attitude-Behavior Theory of Reasoned Action to understand science teachers' attitudes towards physics, computer simulations and inquiry-based experiments*. Paper presented at the Sixth International Conference on Computer Based Learning in Science, University of Cyprus, Nicosia.

Chapter 7
Information Systems' Models for Success Assessment

7.1 Introduction

Information technology (IT) has become one of the most fundamental pillars of modern organizations, and as such, investment on this particular field has steadily grown. Through information systems (IS), networks have been established that allow individuals and organizations to interact through software and hardware, providing the needed link between IT and its users.

The increasing demand of IS has led organizations to become growingly concerned with the effectiveness of such systems. The financial incumbency that they represent requires the delivery of various benefits, in order to be justified, particularly in more dire economic conditions. Entities using IS are moving past the conventional pecuniary metrics that are used to assess IS success, for example, return for the investments made. They are more committed to metrics that are able to provide a more extensive evaluation of the gains of IS employment, such as scorecards and benchmarking. Also, the development of several models to measure success, by the research community, has reiterated the necessity for the growth of quality and consistency in IS success assessment (Petter et al. 2008).

IS success assessment is an essential component of strategic planning within organizational management, compounded by the fact that today's business models have evolved from simple vertical integration, to horizontal interconnectedness between different components, through outsourcing and similar methods (Bechor et al. 2010). Strategic information system planning (SISP) bridges the gap between top management, IT management, and business management, and it is not a fixed set of tools, but an ever evolving one that forms part of an organization's overall strategy development. It has led to the creation of the CIO figure, the Chief Information Officer, around which SISP can be at least somewhat centralized (Abu Bakar et al. 2009). This reality further highlights the necessity for the development of tools and mechanisms to evaluate IS effectiveness.

IS are designed for particular reasons and their success depends greatly on their purpose. An IS' success is relative due to all the elements it entails. The effectiveness that top management finds in an IS may not be seen by the remaining stakeholders. On top of that, IS designers greatly depend on knowing exactly what their goal is, and comparative research on IS success that is based on solid criteria can be of great assistance both in designing the system, and in aiding the client's assessment of whether the system is up to their needs (Palmius 2007).

Therefore, when assessing an IS, it is important to isolate the different points of view and the manners in which all the users are affected (Palmius 2007). Furthermore, IS success measurement research shares the same predicament as many other scientific theories and models, which is external validity. External validity is paramount to research as it determines its capacity to be generalized to different settings. When considering the international application of IS success models, it is important to assess their external validity and their capacity to be used to explain other realities across borders (Agourram 2009).

The area of IS success assessment in constantly challenged and it remains problematic, mainly due to the complexity of the subject, as well as the great number of variables that can be involved in it, and influence it. Also, the fact that work practices are currently so intertwined intricate the separation of their own effects in IS success. It becomes harder to isolate each of their specific impacts, and thus, it becomes harder to evaluate their relevancy in future planning. There is a "fundamental gap in both practical and academic thinking about systems lack of consensus and clarity about the meaning of success where information systems are concerned." (Agourram 2009).

Researchers have tried to overcome this gap, and IS success is broadly considered the dominant metric for IS assessment inside the IS research community (Rai et al. 2002). Early attempts to establish models that explained and simplified why some IS seem to be more successful than others, turned to user acceptance as the defining criterion. However, despite the fact that acceptance is a prerequisite for IS success, it does not equal success (Petter et al. 2008). It is merely a factor.

The intricacy, interdependence, and multi-dimensionality of IS success's nature is at the origin of many failed attempts to outline IS success models (Petter et al. 2008). There are several models that provide a framework for the measurement of IS success, nonetheless their approaches and reach present a variety that hinders the cross comparison of studies and the creation of cumulative research (Sedera and Gable 2004).

7.2 Delone and McLean's IS Success Model

In 1992, DeLone and McLean proposed a taxonomy of IS success categories, arguing that "if information systems research is to make a contribution to the world of practice, a well-defined outcome measure (or measures) is essential" (DeLone and McLean 1992). The variety of measures used in prior studies led the authors to

7.2 Delone and McLean's IS Success Model

try and obtain a simpler pattern or patterns of measures by compiling existing studies and evaluating the measures used in them.

Their model proposed a framework to determine IS success that encompassed six categories: "System quality, information quality, use, user satisfaction, individual impact, and organizational impact" (DeLone and McLean 1992; Petter et al. 2008). The D&M model is based on the notion that the quality of both the system and the information has an impact on users' satisfaction and usage. This model defends the interdependency between usage and user satisfaction (Iivari 2005) and is primarily a causal-explanatory model, describing how use and user satisfaction, reciprocally affecting each other, directly influence individual impact, and how individual impact in turn translates into organizational impact (Iivari 2005) (Fig. 7.1).

The original D&M model was updated in 2003 and it included a new dimension: service quality. The updated model was then composed of six success dimensions: systems quality, information quality, service quality, system use, user satisfaction, and net benefits (Petter et al. 2008).

System quality accounts for the ideal features of an IS, such as usability, reliability, and response time. It measures technical success. *Information quality* concerns the outputs of the system and their ideal traits. The system is expected to have concise, relevant, and accurate outcomes. Management reports and Web pages are some of the possible outcomes of the system. The authors define this as "semantic success" (DeLone and McLean 2003). *Service quality*, introduced with the model's revision, corresponds to the quality of the support that the users benefit from. It is the degree and quality of the IT support available to the user. It measures aspects such as the responsiveness, technical competence, and empathy. The SERVQUAL instrument has been used and widely accepted as a measurement tool for service quality in IS, but despite its value it is a restrictive tool, as it only contemplates service quality, which is just one of the many elements of an IS (Palmius 2007). Nevertheless, service quality's growing relevancy over the last

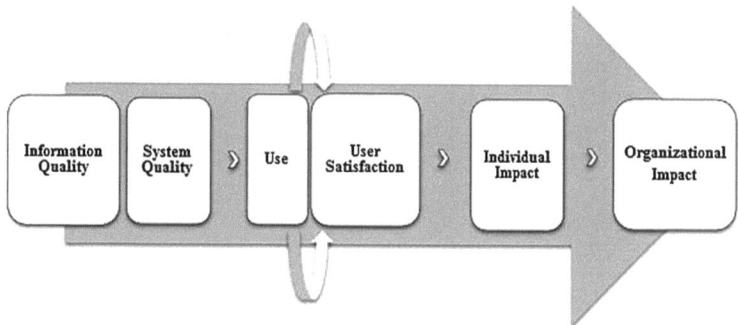

Fig. 7.1 DeLone and McLean's original model of IS success (adapted from DeLone and McLean 1992)

decades, along with the changes to IS use, namely end user computing, justify the inclusion of service quality as its own, separate category (DeLone and McLean 2003).

System use assesses the way the system is used and how its features are harnessed by users, both staff members and clients. It evaluates, among other elements, the frequency and amount of use, the purpose of the use and the nature of the use. In terms of user satisfaction, the objective of this dimension is to measure the degree of satisfaction with the overall characteristics, outcomes, and support services of the system.

The updated D&M model also substitutes the two dimensions of impact (individual and organizational) for the larger concept of *net benefits*, in order to include a wider population, such as groups, industries, and countries. The increase in productivity, the creation of jobs, or the economical development are some of the criteria used to assess the net benefits to a panoply of entities (Petter et al. 2008). Some models of IS success assessment prefer to dissect the variables into subvariables, or simply increment the number of success variables, but the D&M model rather simplifies the list of IS categories. Therefore, by transforming the two impact categories into "net benefits," the model becomes open to allow for a particular determination of who is affected by the IS. By using the net benefits label, the model endows each individual process of IS success measurement to determine what type of impact it will consider (individual, organizational, national, and departmental) (DeLone 2003) (Fig. 7.2).

The original D&M model for IS success contributed with five core premises.

First, it is paramount to account for the fact that IS have an interdependent and multidimensional nature, which means one will have to pay attention to the interactions between the several success dimensions.

Second, while tested and empirically validated measures are ideal, the success of IS should be determined according to the particular aims and context of the IS.

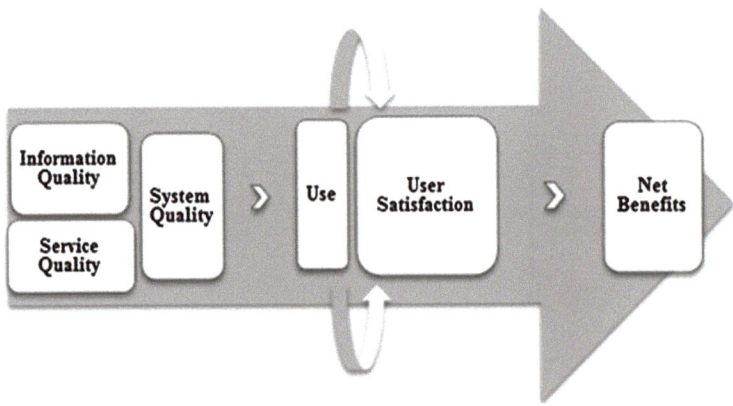

Fig. 7.2 DeLone and McLean's updated model of IS success (adapted from DeLone and McLean 1992)

Third, the multiplicity of success measures should be reduced to a minimum to increase the possibilities of comparing studies and enhance the opportunity to validate them.

Fourth, the organizational impact criteria for IS success assessment are undervalued and under-researched.

And fifth, there is evident need for improvement of the original D&M model (Delone 2003).

The research work that originated the D&M IS success model reviewed 180 studies concerning IS success measurement. In this review, the diversity of IS success markers became clear. The six categories proposed in the paper served as a classification criteria for all the IS success methods in the 180 studies. Hence, the authors found that some studies concentrated their efforts in system quality, by exploring the features of the IS that were required to guarantee its quality. The focus of some of the studies was placed in the information quality, in criteria such as timeliness and accuracy. An approach that also became evident was that of the systems' interaction with their users. In this case, the emphasis was directed at the use of the system and the satisfaction of its users. The final views of IS success assessment concern the impact that the system has at an individual level, in management decision making and at an organizational level, in the performance of the organization itself (DeLone and McLean 1992). One of the conclusions of the D&M model was the lack of research on measures that contemplated the impact of IS on an organizational level (DeLone and McLean 2002).

One of the most important aspects of the D&M model is the fact that it provided a taxonomy to categorize the wide variety of criteria used in IS success assessment. It organized the different measures into a framework of six dimensions. Also, while outlining this framework, the model established a "temporal and causal" relation between its several measures (Seddon 1997). Although the dimensions of success and their metrics should be adjusted to specific objectives and contexts, it is important to choose measures that have been tested and validated (DeLone and McLean 2002).

The D&M model provides a framework for the assessment of IS success both at the individual and organizational levels. Nonetheless, when moving past utilitarian IS, this model has yet to prove its adequacy regarding IS that are related to enjoyment and leisure. The dimensions that are used in this model to measure IS success have not yet prove their pertinence in terms of social networking, gaming environments, or any other IS that was designed for entertainment, in general. In order to extend this model to this type of IS, it may be necessary to review some of its criteria (Petter et al. 2008).

When outlining the D&M model, the authors made clear that the model was a work in progress that further research and validation was required (DeLone and McLean 2002).

7.3 Seddon Model

The Seddon's model presented itself as both an extension and a restructuring of the D&M model (Seddon 1997). Seddon believed that the D&M model made important contributions to IS success measurement, but it was overly ambitious, which caused it to suffer from lack of clarity and misspecification (Seddon 1997). According to him, the model presented two main shortcomings: the fact that the model integrated causal relationship explanations as well as process relationship explanations, a puzzling combination; and the ambiguity of the employment of "use" as a dimension, which is also unsuitable for causal relationships explanations. Seddon then attempted to resolve both issues within his own framework (Rabaa'i and Gable 2009).

There are two parts in the conceptual foundation of the Seddon's model: a behavioral structure of IS usage, and the IS success framework itself. According to the author, the D&M model was unclear, by oversimplifying concepts and mixing both categories together. The graphical representation of the D&M model itself was ambiguous, as various meanings could be attributed to the relationships depicted in that graphic (arrows and boxes). It was, therefore, fundamental to split the model into two variance submodels, *use* and *success*, thus eliminating the simple, one-directional process interpretation of the D&M model (Seddon 1997) (Fig. 7.3).

The *behavioral structure* outlines the argument that the expectations of users with regard to IS have great repercussions in the success of IS. Individuals' expectations determine how they will see the system's success and the criteria they will employ to measure that success. Hence, user expectations and IS use fall under this first part of the model. Whereas the D&M model implies that system quality, information quality, and user satisfaction are all part of a causal relationship that allows to directly predict the future IS use, Seddon argues that how well a system has done in the past is not the only reason behind its usage, and introduces the fundamental concept of expectation as a key variable. No matter how satisfied a user is with a given system, if that user expects a new system to do much better, he or she will use it. Thus, the behavioral model of IS use consists primarily of a one-way relationship that starts with *expectations about the net benefits of future IS use*, leading to *IS use* itself (Seddon 1997).

The second part, the IS success structure, is close to the D&M model as it identifies three different categories of IS success measures (Kurian et al. 2000): "measures of information and systems quality, perceptual measures of usefulness

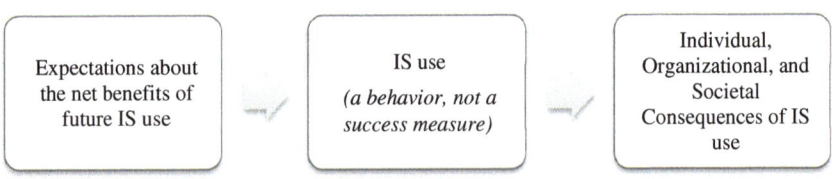

Fig. 7.3 Behavioral model of IS use (adapted from Seddon 1997)

7.3 Seddon Model

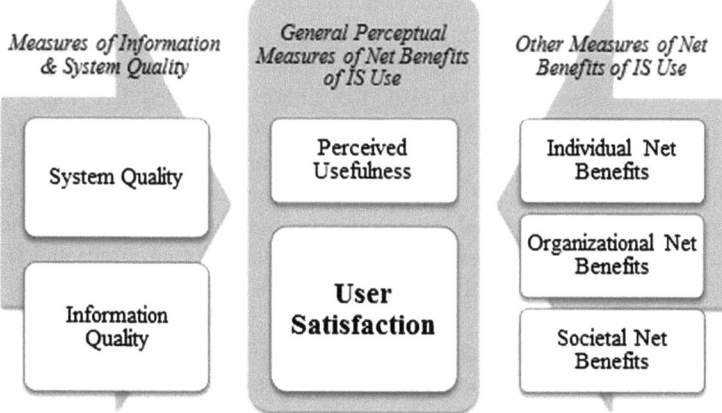

Fig. 7.4 IS success model (adapted from Seddon 1997)

and satisfaction, and measures of net benefits to individuals, organisations and society" (p. 3).

According to the Seddon's model, IS use is not assessed as either good or bad. It is regarded as a *behavior* and not a success measurement criteria (Kurian et al. 2000).

Both submodels are interconnected via one factor, which is *user satisfaction* (Fig. 7.4). The variables *system quality, information quality, perceived usefulness*, and *net benefits to individuals, organizations and society*—all provide influence upon user satisfaction, which, in turn, defines the expectations about future use, and thus influence IS use itself. This feedback stream means user satisfaction is a significant component of Seddon's model, though not a success measure as in the D&M model.

However, similarly to the D&M model's approach, we can isolate here five core aspects: *System quality, information quality, perceived usefulness, user satisfaction,* and *IS usage*. In this model, the relationship between these core elements is clarified in order to provide a better understanding of how they work together and create success. The quality of the system and the quality of the information have repercussions at the level of perceived usefulness and user satisfaction. Users' perceived usefulness will affect user satisfaction, which in turn influence the use of a system. Hence, the fact that a system has good quality, that the information is equally good, will leave the users with the perception that the system will be useful. If the system is perceived as being helpful, the user will be satisfied and that causes him/her to use the system (Lin 2008).

In 1999, Seddon, Staples, Patnayakuni, and Bowtell further expanded the above model, by outlining an *IS effectiveness matrix*. They then tested it, by using the matrix to classify IS effectiveness measures from 186 empirical papers published over the course of 9 years. The matrix was a two-dimensional equation consisting of two factors: the type of IS studied, and the stakeholder in whose interests the system is being evaluated. Each stakeholder has different demands for the IS, so it is necessary to understand that their specific role will determine what they will outline as success measures (Seddon et al. 1999).

Regarding the *stakeholder* variable, the authors identified five major groups whose points of view were generally used in related studies: the *independent observer*, who is distant from the process and therefore is not accounted as a stakeholder; the *individual user*, who wishes to grow positively; a *group of people*, who, similarly to the individual, also wants to improve their situation; the *management team*, whose aims regard the success of their organization; and finally *a specific country*, whose objective is the general well-being and progress of the society.

The *system* variable refers to the specificities of the system being evaluated. Depending on a series of components, the success measurement will be conducted differently. Studies generally resorted to the following six dimensions: just *one item of the system*, such as its user interface; *one individual IT application* inside the entity, such as a computer; *a particular type of application*, for instance a data warehouse; *all the IT applications* that an entity or a group within an entity uses, for example, all the IT applications used in a marketing department; *a part of the system development procedure*, such as design or reengineering; and finally, *the IT management* in an entity (Seddon et al. 1999).

If the success of an IS was to be measured under these two perspectives, there would be thirty possible combinations, and hence, thirty resulting criteria to evaluate the success. Considering, for example, that success of all the IT applications of a certain organization was going to be measured from the point of view of the management team, what the assessment process would be looking for was a growth in sales, increased productivity, and revenue (Seddon et al. 1999). The possible combinations are illustrated in the Table 7.1.

With this system, the authors attempted to present another alternative to the D&M model, by lowering the importance of defining a "comprehensive measurement instrument" (DeLone and McLean 1992), and instead emphasizing the importance of identifying the *context* in which IS effectiveness is being evaluated (Seddon et al. 1999).

Kurian et al. (2000) later proposed an extension of the Seddon's model, arguing that the constant, dynamic evolution of IS called for regular and appropriate updates to existing models, in what they defined as "rapid adaptation." As a result, they introduced into the model two fundamental elements: *group impact* and *external impact*.

Group impact is a measure that accounts for the insertion of the individual using the IS in a specific group. The group impact is felt through the interaction of the IS user with his/her peers. Groups can assume different shapes and they include structures that are already in place, such as specific departments, or an ad hoc assembly of people to meet certain goals, such as a team. The authors argue that there is a variety of impacts that fall under this category that were not specified by other categories in both the D&M and the Seddon's models, such as: number of ideas raised, degree of participation, reduction in social pressure, group think, group

7.3 Seddon Model

Table 7.1. Some examples of different combinations of system and stakeholder (adapted from Seddon et al. 1999)

Stakeholder interest group	An aspect of IT use	A single IT application	A type of IT application	All IT applications	An aspect of system development	An IT function
Independent observer	Accuracy or speed of algorithm	Performance outcome expectations	Communication effectiveness	Cumulative abnormal returns following IT investment announcements	Accuracy and consistency of software estimates	Important skills for EIS developers from survey or current practices
Individual	User acceptance of expert system advice	Creative performance	Work–Family conflicts due to work-related home computer use	Self-rated job performance	User satisfaction consequence of participation	Service quality
Group	Post-meeting consensus		Equality of participation, perceived group performance			
Management	Perceived usefulness computer-based information	Price premium per gallon for fuel sold via the Cardlock system	Reduced inventory holding costs, reduced premium fright costs	Sales growth, ROA, labor productivity	Cost savings, quality improvement, customer satisfaction	Benefits to the firm flowing from IT outsourcing
Country			Evaluation of electronic market for computerized loan origination	Productivity and consumer surplus		*Not applicable*

consensus, group efficiency, awareness of others, group cohesion, conflict in group, and change in work habits. The significance of these impacts was reduced as they were lumped into oversimplifying variables, such as organizational impact, that did not take into account the specificity of group impact, which often does not directly affect the entire organization (Kurian et al. 2000).

External impact considers the world outside of the organization which is using the IS, by emphasizing the use of external information technology (EIT) that allows for information exchange between the organization and the outside world. This very significant form of global networking has become a major aspect of IS application. It endows institutions with the capacity to be free from time and space restrains. Some research elements that had been previously used and could fall under this category are the sustainability of IT-based competitiveness, inter-organizational systems, electronic markets, global information systems, data networks, private industry networks, the Internet, etc. However, the authors point out that despite its significance and the existence of these research variables, there was never an explicit acknowledgment of external impact as a category in itself, and its role in IS success measure (Kurian et al. 2000).

By including these two categories, the authors aimed to enhance the Seddon's model to account for the specificities of the net benefits of "group-oriented systems and from external-oriented systems" (Kurian et al. 2000).

7.4 3D Model of Information Systems Success

In 1996, Ballantine, Bonner, Levy, Martin, Munro, and Powell attempted to develop the D&M model further, acknowledging that this model was the standard that many researchers either adopted or attempted to improve. The authors detected a number of aspects in Delone and McLean's research that needed revising, such as the lack of clarification on which were the dependent and independent variables, and on whether their study aimed at being a taxonomy, a framework, or a model. They also reached a similar conclusion as Seddon in that certain concepts were oversimplified, for example, using the concept of quality without regard to the intended purpose of the system.

Ballantine et al. thus attempted to present a richer and more complete study of the overall impact of IS, by developing a model that focused on the process through which IS are implemented, and how the global system's success can be measured at each one of the levels of that process.

The 3D model divided the notion of IS success into three primordial aspects or stages: "the technical development level, the deployment to the user, and the delivery of business benefits." (Ballantine et al. 1996). The 3D model denomination came from these three core stages of IS creation: **d**evelopment, **d**eployment, and **d**elivery.

The *development stage* concerns the creation of an IS. The development of the system starts ideally after a study on strategy or viability. The successful outcome

7.4 3D Model of Information Systems Success

of this period is dependent on a variety of factors, namely the quality of the technology, the project management and the data, the intricacy of the system, user involvement, and the professional competences of the developers (Ballantine et al. 1996).

Deployment is initiated once the system is fully developed and it refers to its implementation in the particular context for which it was designed. The implementation phase proves that regardless of a system's technical quality, its acceptance by the users will dictate its success or failure. If, for example, the use of the system is compulsory rather than voluntary, this will also invalidate its proliferation in the deployment phase and consequently in the delivery (Ballantine et al. 1996).

To complete the three stages, *delivery* happens when the system has been implemented and it is ready to accomplish the objectives for which it was intended.

Between each level, there are filters that act upon the three stages and can inhibit or encourage the adoption of the system at each stage. These filters are described as *implementation*, acting between development and deployment; *integration*, acting between deployment and delivery; and *environment*, acting upon delivery. Possible factors of implementation are user involvement and expectations, user experience, and whether the system is mandatory or discretionary. Possible factors of integration are strategy, organizational culture, and organizational structure. Possible factors of environment are competitor movements, economic, and political context (Ballantine et al. 1996). Some of these factors are exogenous, as in they are completely independent factors that develop outside the system (Fig. 7.5).

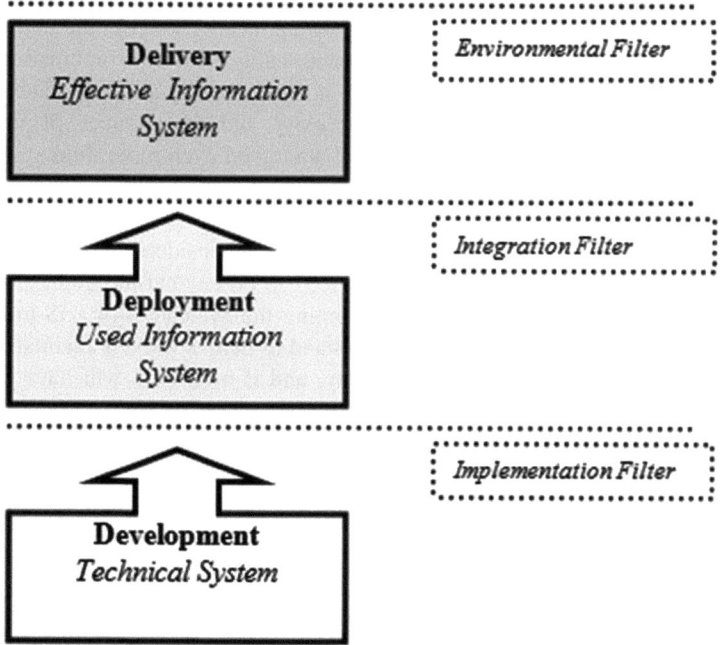

Fig. 7.5 The 3D model of IS success (adapted from Ballantine et al. 1996)

A fundamental aspect of this model is that success in the development and deployment levels are insufficient to guarantee the system's overall success. The system may not be able to deliver due to the organization's structure or lack of cultural recognition of information technology's value. Hence, the system will succeed if it is integrated in the company. In its turn, this integration is conditioned by a multiplicity of conditions, for instance, the support of senior management, the people operating the system, and flexible structural organization. "At the delivery level, the issues and forces are not particularly IS-oriented; they are forces which are at work in any change process which aims to enhance business performance." (Ballantine et al. 1996). Thus, the delivery stage includes factors that are not exclusively concerned with IS per se, but with the general organization and culture of a company and its employees.

With the 3D model, the authors have also introduced the concept of a learning feedback loop that develops alongside the process of IS developing. If IS are presented as a 3-stage process of growth, the learning feedback loop is what determines the curve from development to delivery and is a key aspect of measuring its success.

7.5 IS-impact Measurement Model

Information systems is an area that is in constant, rapid development, and thus many researchers have pointed out the need for reevaluation and restructuring of older, traditional models. Organizations are comprised of a multitude of users, from top executives to data entry operators; various applications across the entire organization; and numerous capabilities and functionality, and the combination of so many factors means that old models might not be properly adjusted (Gable et al. 2008). Emphasizing this aspect of complexity and the number of variables involved, other models were developed that attempted even more fluid systems of measures. An example is the IS-impact measurement model that was developed in a study by authors Gable, Sedera, and Chan.

The IS-impact measurement model takes into consideration the long-term investment that IS represent. It argues the need to go beyond the traditional measures of impact assessment. Rather than limiting the evaluation of a IS to its past and current impact, it is paramount to understand if there is value in maintaining the system, if it needs to be altered in any way, and if its impact will have positive repercussions in the future. The assessment of an IS success should account both for the past (its impact) and the future (its quality). Hence, the IS-impact measurement model has two main branches: *impact*, which represent the ramification of the system so far; and *quality*, which stands for the effects that the system is expected to have (Gable et al. 2008).

The IS-impact model evaluates the success of an IS according to four guidelines:

- *Information quality* refers to the quality of the information that is created;
- *System quality* concerns a more technical approach; it regards the performance of the system itself;

7.5 IS-impact Measurement Model

- *Individual impact* refers to the effect that the system has on individual users;
- *Organizational impact* accounts for the effect the system produces on a particular organization (Alkhalaf et al. 2013).

These five dimensions of success measurement are not related through causality processes, and this represents a major difference from the Delone and McLean model. Instead, those five dimensions are correlated with the global concept of IS success, as variables that contribute to it, rather than being the cause of it. It is a measurement structure, not a process (Fig. 7.6).

The five core components of this model each entail a series of measures, the instrument with which success is measured across the full scale of activity within the organization—management, user-base, and technical. This model can thus be used as a set of guidelines to compare different enterprise systems versions and also to establish a comparison between organizations or departments (Rabaa'i and Gable 2009).

Another notable aspect of this model is that it does not account for system use as one of the metrics. Indeed, the authors argue that system use might not be a valid measure on a number of occasions, namely in organizations where such use is mandatory, and therefore is not dependent on other factors such as satisfaction or expectation. We had previously seen Seddon et al. making a similar argument, but whereas the Seddon's model placed system use as a component of its behavioral submodel, here the variable is simply removed for further clarity.

User satisfaction, on the other hand, is introduced in this model as one of the several criteria for the evaluation of success, instead of defining it as a success construct in itself. However, both use and user satisfaction are conceptualized further as external variables to the finalized model.

This finalized model, as mentioned above, emphasizes the dichotomy between impact and quality as the fundamental keystones of success measurement, on equal footing. The five core components outlined in the conceptual model are thus integrated in this scheme where impacts to date and future impacts are part of a fluid dynamic.

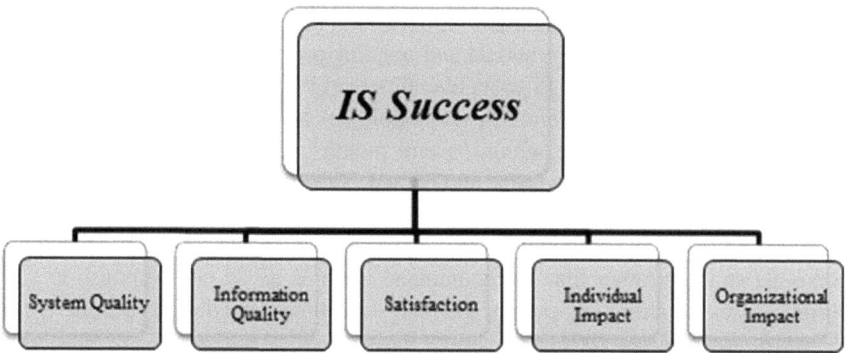

Fig. 7.6 The conceptual basis for the IS-impact measurement model (adapted from Gable et al. 2008)

The IS-impact model introduced new measures of success to consider recent IS settings and organizational features. It "includes additional measures to probe a more holistic organizational impacts construct" (Gable et al. 2003). Since the IS-impact model provides measures that are meaningful to all the stakeholders of IS, it becomes possible to compare their different perceptions. This feature also allows for a combination of their views (Rabaa'i and Gable 2009).

The question of the external validity of this model has been empirically tested throughout several studies and it remains a focus in ongoing research. Rabaa'i and Gable (2009) started a study that aimed to employ the IS-impact measurement in the context of higher education administrative systems. Their study is ongoing and it examining Australasian universities in particular. They are trying to establish an empirical base for this IS success model in a different context (Rabaa'i and Gable 2009). Their results will add to the current body of research and it will attest the capacity of generalization of the IS-impact measurement system.

7.6 Strategic Information Systems Planning (SISP) Effectiveness

Strategic Information Systems Planning (SISP) has been increasingly emphasized by researchers as a growing key aspect of IS research, as it fundamentally correlates with the role of IS on the strategic direction of the organization itself. As technology becomes paramount to success in a competitive environment, IS planning becomes an essential component of growth and successful competition.

The concept of SISP has been discussed since 1970s, but it has seen a steady evolution due to the accompanying technological progress: the Internet, personal computers, outsourcing, and user applications are all factors that have contributed to the expansion of IS from a closed subgroup to a necessary tool of interaction and cooperation with external variables, and this expansion has made SISP more relevant, and thus, more actively researched.

Authors Newkirk and Lederer defined SISP as the process of determining an institution's assortment of computer applications that can contribute to attain its own mission. It is an entirely rational and ongoing process managed on the basis of adjusting the organization's IS to its overall strategy (Newkirk and Lederer 2007). This process entails the selection of methodologies and an IS planners committee, and it generally takes place within several months. SISP procedures need a significant investment in terms of time and budget. They imply diverse tasks that allow organizations to prioritize IS development (Abu Bakar et al. 2009). It is a "rational process, intended to recommend new information systems linked to an overall corporate strategy rather than to recommend them as an ad hoc response to such current crises as shrinking profits, growing lead-times and falling productivity." (Newkirk and Lederer 2007).

7.6 Strategic Information Systems Planning (SISP) Effectiveness

There are five stages in SISP: strategic awareness, situation analysis, strategy conception, strategy formulation, and strategy implementation (Newkirk and Lederer 2007).

Strategic awareness is the seminal stage in which key planning issues are defined through team meetings and top management committees. *Situation analysis* allows for the examination of the context and available systems at the moment of planning. *Strategy conception* then implies establishing the objectives and pinpointing where the systems can be improved in order to facilitate those objectives. *Strategy formulation* is the shaping of the strategy, through new business processes, IT architectures and more specific projects. Finally, *strategy implementation* is when action and management plans are defined, as well as follow-up and control procedures (Newkirk and Lederer 2007) (Fig. 7.7).

SISP is widely accepted as a success model for IS, nonetheless, there are two core elements of its approach that have been given insufficient accentuation: planning process and planning progress. In order to demonstrate how companies can potentiate the effectiveness and reap the benefits of their trust in SISP, it is paramount to understand the planning process and the way in which it is attained. Also, it becomes essential to monitor the evolution of the planning process, to see how it changes through its different stages (Grover and Segars 2005). Finally, it is essential to understand how SISP can be improved and what elements are vital to its effectiveness.

According to authors Bechor et al. (2010), there are three main categories under which it is possible to place the variables involved in determining SISP success: key success factors, planning approach, and planning context.

Key success factors account for the required conditions to ensure SISP's success, such as user participation. However, the authors add that it is not possible to predict SISP success based solely on these factors, which need to be integrated in a wider model comprised of more variables.

The *planning approach* concerns the style of the planning itself. It refers to the different angles that may guide the planning process, defining its timeline and focus, often through a commercial perspective.

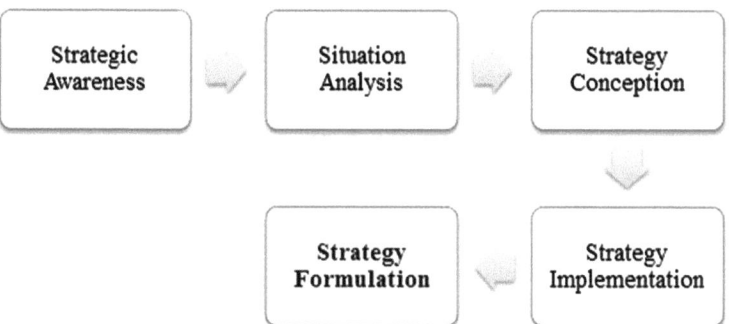

Fig. 7.7 Process of strategic information systems planning, according to Newkirk and Lederer (2007)

Finally, the *planning context* is composed of all the variables that stand for the different features of the organization and its context such as variables of external conditions and environmental impacts such as the economic scenario or the organizational structure. Context is a fundamental key aspect that was often ignored in research (Bechor et al. 2010).

Through the use of multiple variables from these three dimensions, the study of SISP becomes multifaceted and more equipped to describing reality, particularly in a world of swift change and evolution. In fact, researchers often point out that SISP has the capacity to *adapt* throughout time. It has the ability to address any changes in terms of environment and technology. It can be constantly improved through the process of learning overtime, and thus constantly adjust to the wider frame of organizational strategy (Grover and Segars 2005).

The swift evolution of the Internet and IT in general has propelled SISP to incorporate several dimensions in its process. SISP moves beyond the elementary aspects of the business strategy and the IT resources of an organization. It presents a much broader equation by considering also the culture, the skill set, the expertise, and the context of an organization. The combination of all these aspects is fundamental to a more complete SISP. Due to the engagement of SISP in all aspects of a company, some have argued that people would benefit from seeing SISP as a learning routine instead of solely regarding it as a solution to a problem (Abu Bakar et al. 2009).

As IT becomes progressively more important to organizations, SISP assumes a central role. Companies resort to SISP to ensure that they are leveraging their IS resources to the maximum. The competitiveness and rapid transformation of the IT sector is thought to enhance the perils of poor planning. In that context, the engagement of senior management in SISP conduces to a better alignment between the business plan and the IS plan (Fergerson 2012).

SISP is regarded as a powerful management instrument and often considered "the best mechanism for assuring that IT activities are congruent with those of the rest of the organization and its evolving needs" (Bechor et al. 2010). When approached as a learning activity, SISP becomes a guide for understanding the company in its entirety. IS planning is more than an outcome of SISP, it is far from being the ultimate document, rather it is important that the organization considers it a guide that will prospectively assist in the drawing of the next plans (Abu Bakar et al. 2009).

SISP success can be determined through five possible outcomes: alignment, analysis, cooperation, improvement in capabilities, and contribution.

Alignment promotes a close link between IS strategy and business strategy. This outcome implies that top management strategies are synchronized with IS strategy and tools, and thus, there is a positive incentive for top management to support and invest in SISP.

Analysis consists of the effort to comprehend the organization's internal routines for technology, process, and procedures. If this process is facilitated it becomes easier to understand the organization's internal processes and architectures, and how it is possible to use IT tools to integrate the organization's information systems and their management in those processes.

7.6 Strategic Information Systems Planning (SISP) Effectiveness

Cooperation is vital to decrease the possibility of conflict when putting in practice the strategic IS plans. All parties are, hence, encouraged to compromise in a general agreement, namely when it comes to defining what are the priorities in terms of development.

Improvement in capabilities refers to the desired outcome of the IS planning, which is its perfection over time and a clear enhancement of its ability to provide the necessary support to the organization, also through a process of learning over time. Ultimately, it is the potential contained in the SISP to the overall betterment of the organizational adaptation process.

Finally, in terms of *contribution*, what is expected from the system planning is its active participation in the effectiveness of the organization in general. SISP's repercussions should be felt throughout the different elements of the organization's effectiveness, such as profitability and decision making (Grover and Segars 2005).

The effort that SISP involves requires its benefits to be extended to several areas of organizational value. Nonetheless, there are insufficient metrics to help in determining the success of SISP and assessing its benefits. That are considerable gains in SISP that remain intangible (Segars and Grover 1998). Although there have been several attempts to quantify the impact that SISP has, "limited theoretical or practical justification is provided for the content of SISP effectiveness measure" (Segars and Grover 1998).

SISP is adopted by private sector entities as well as by public sector institutions that are faced with the mounting intricacy of their IT structures and that are pressured by their users' demand of high-quality service (Abu Bakar et al. 2009) (Fig. 7.8).

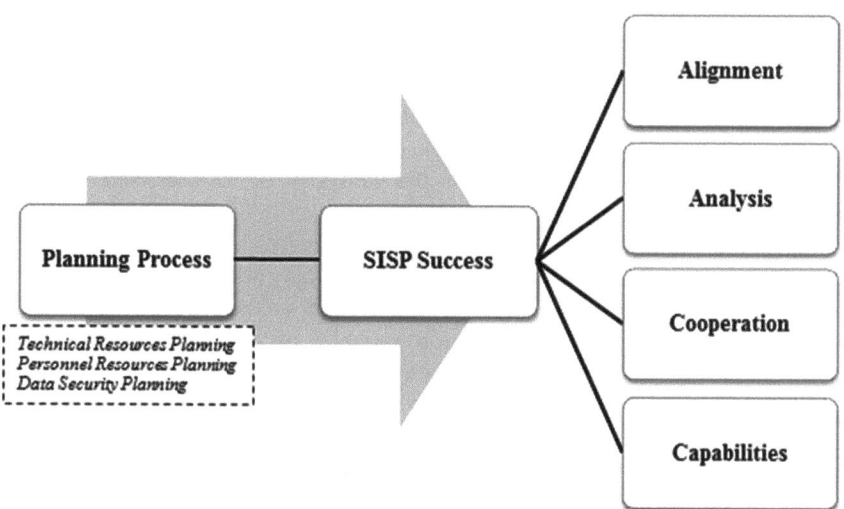

Fig. 7.8 A model for SISP success (adapted from Newkirk and Lederer 2007)

7.7 Other Models for IS Success Evaluation

We have previously summarized and outlined the most significant models used in IS success research. However, the attempt to identify and systemically analyze success variables is an ongoing academic process, and there have been other models and frameworks outlined on the basis of research and literature reviews.

The work system method of IS success measurement, or WSM, was developed by Alter in 1999 in an attempt to bring IS success measurement closer to business practices. This method combines two dimensions: a static dimension called the work system framework, which outlines the basic architecture of the organization, and a dynamic one called the work system life cycle. This life cycle is the process through which any new system is implemented in an organization and consists of four stages: initiation, development, implementation, and operation maintenance. At the level of operation maintenance, there is a component of performance monitoring and eventual identification and correction of issues. It is at this stage that success of the new system is evaluated, which in turn will have an impact on whether the system will be continued, adapted, or rejected (Lawrence 2011).

Davis and subsequent co-authors the concept of a technology acceptance model (TAM) for the purpose of modeling user acceptance of information systems, seen as a fundamental aspect of success. Much like the Seddon's model, the emphasis is on perceived usefulness and perceived ease of use, two factors that, combined with external variables, will influence the attitude toward use and, in turn, determine actual usage (Zaied 2012).

Zaied later structured a method for the evaluation of IS success by combining elements from the theoretical foundations of the TAM and of the D&M model update (Zaied 2012). The IS success model that the author suggests is composed of ten variables: "behavior intentions, information quality, management support, perceived ease of use, perceived usefulness, service quality, system quality, training, user satisfaction, and user involvement." This list of variables portrays a clear integration of the D&M model's dimensions from its updated version with TAM's core precepts (Zaied 2012). However, this model proposed a more strict concept of IS success by focusing exclusively on the viewpoint of the user, and it did not account for other stakeholders (Zaied 2012).

Agourram has argued that culture is an increasingly significant determinant of the manner that people perceive IS success. Particularly with the explosive growth of cross-cultural organizations and multinational IS architectures, there is necessarily a significant influence of cultural variables on modern research models. Hence, there are many researchers that contest the wide applicability of existing IS success models because many of them do not take into account such variables, or relegate them to a secondary plane. However, the reality is that different contexts and cultures demand specific approaches, and there is more evidence today to contradict the preconceived idea of universal applicability of IT. When an organization is set on a multinational environment, culture has to be given a predominant place in that organization's success measurement model (Agourram 2009).

7.8 Conclusions

Research on IS success measurement is a vast body of knowledge without a single methodology or framework that can be universally applied.

DeLone and McLean outlined a model that relied primarily on the concept of a process of causal relationships, comprised of three major key aspects: quality, use, and impact. Their seminal work, which was far from defining a complete and comprehensive model for future studies, merely opened the door for progress on that field, and there have been numerous attempts to improve that model, or to create a new one.

The Seddon's model worked on the D&M concept even further and defended the notion that the behavioral aspect of IS use must be emphasized as it fundamentally alters the simple causal processes described by D&M. It also brought attention to the need to further examine the concept of impact, which D&M had outlined as a simple dual concept of organizational and individual impact. Seddon introduced the concepts of net benefits and expectations as part of the success cycle.

The 3D model attempted to shift the focus of research toward the process of IS development and implementation, arguing that it is along this process that measures for success can be identified, implemented, and used in an ongoing learning cycle.

The IS-impact measurement model went back to the D&M approach and again emphasized a duality of quality and impact as key factors of success, but built a more fluid, dynamic correlation between those factors.

Generically, we can see that researchers have all agreed in that IS success cannot be estimated with accurate precision because it relies on multiple variables, some external to the system, other endogenous to it. The degree of importance attributed to these variables can differ greatly from study to study; however, some factors have been recurrently used, such as usage and user satisfaction. However, different studies will insert these factors within different processes and/or cycles.

Ultimately, IS success measurement research is a field that will, most likely, continuously grow and evolve as IT and IS itself evolves, because it is a fundamental and necessary aspect of modern organizational management in a technologically driven, globalized world.

References

Abu Bakar, F., Suhaimi, M. A., & Hussin, H. (2009). *Conceptualization of Strategic Information Systems Planning (SISP) success model in public sector: An absorptive capacity approach.* Paper presented at the European and Mediterranean Conference on Information Systems 2009 (EMCIS 2009), Izmir, Turkey.

Agourram, H. (2009). Defining information system success in Germany. *International Journal of Information Management, 29*(2), 129–137.

Alkhalaf, S., Drew, S., & Nguyen, A. (2013). Validation of the IS Impact Model for measuring the impact of e-learning systems in KSA universities: Student perspective. *International Journal of Advanced Computer Science and Applications, 3*(5), 71–76.

Ballantine, J., Bonner, M., Levy, M., Martin, A., Munro, I., & Powell, P. (1996). The 3-D model of information systems success: The search for the dependent variable continues. *Information Resources Management Journal, 9*(4), 5–15.

Bechor, T., Neumann, S., Zviran, M., & Glezer, C. (2010). A contingency model for estimating success of strategic information systems planning. *Information & Management, 47*(1), 17–29.

Delone, W. H. (2003). The DeLone and McLean model of information systems success: A ten-year update. *Journal of management information systems, 19*(4), 9–30.

DeLone, W. H., and McLean, E. R. (1992). Information systems success: The quest for the dependent variable. *Information Systems Research, 3*(1), 60–95.

DeLone, W. H., and McLean, E. R. (2002). *Information systems success revisited.* Paper presented at the 35th Annual Hawaii International Conference on System Sciences, HICSS 2002.

Fergerson, B. (2012). *Key stages of Strategic Information System Planning (SISP) methods and alignment to strategic management planning concepts.* Presented to the Interdisciplinary Studies Program, University of Oregon.

Gable, G. G., Sedera, D., & Chan, T. (2003). Enterprise systems success: A measurement model. *ICIS 2003 Proceedings, paper 48.*

Gable, G. G., Sedera, D., & Chan, T. (2008). Re-conceptualizing information system success: The IS-impact measurement model. *Journal of the association for information systems, 9*(7), 377–408.

Grover, V., & Segars, A. H. (2005). An empirical evaluation of stages of strategic information systems planning: patterns of process design and effectiveness. *Information & Management, 42*(5), 761–779.

Iivari, J. (2005). An empirical test of the DeLone-McLean model of information system success. *ACM SIGMIS Database, 36*(2), 8–27.

Kurian, D., Gallupe, R., & Diaz, J. (2000). *Taking stock: Measuring information systems success.* Paper presented at the Administrative Sciences Association of Canada—Annual Conference.

Lawrence, R. (2011). *A Comparison of the DeLone and McLean Model of IS Success and the Work System Method: Three Field Studies in Healthcare Organizations* (Doctoral dissertation). Retrieved from https://repositories.tdl.org/ttu-ir/bitstream/handle/2346/ETD-TTU-2011-05-1549/LAWRENCE-DISSERTATION.pdf?sequence=2

Lin, H.-F. (2008). Antecedents of virtual community satisfaction and loyalty: An empirical test of competing theories. *CyberPsychology & Behavior, 11*(2), 138–144.

Newkirk, H. E., & Lederer, A. L. (2007). The effectiveness of strategic information systems planning for technical resources, personnel resources, and data security in environments of heterogeneity and hostility. *Journal of Computer Information Systems, 47*(3), 34–44.

Palmius, J. (2007). *Criteria for measuring and comparing information systems.* Paper presented at the 30th Information Systems Research Seminar in Scandinavia (IRIS-30).

Petter, S., DeLone, W., and McLean, E. (2008). Measuring information systems success: Models, dimensions, measures, and interrelationships. *European Journal of Information Systems, 17*(3), 236–263.

Rabaa'i, A. A., & Gable, G. G. (2009). *Extending the IS-Impact Model into the higher education sector.* Paper presented at the ICICS2009: 7th International Conference on Information and Communications Systems.

Rai, A., Lang, S. S., & Welker, R. B. (2002). Assessing the validity of IS success models: An empirical test and theoretical analysis. *Information Systems Research, 13*(1), 50–69.

Seddon, P. B. (1997). A respecification and extension of the DeLone and McLean model of IS success. *Information Systems Research, 8*(3), 240–253.

Seddon, P. B., Staples, S., Patnayakuni, R., & Bowtell, M. (1999). Dimensions of information systems success. *Communications of the AIS, 2*(3es), article 5.

Sedera, D., & Gable, G. G. (2004). A factor and structural equation analysis of the enterprise systems success measurement model. *ICIS 2004 Proceedings*, pp. 449–464.

Segars, A. H., & Grover, V. (1998). Strategic information systems planning success: An investigation of the constructs and its measurement. *MIS Quarterly, 22*(2), 139–163.

Zaied, A. N. H. (2012). An integrated success model for evaluating information system in public sectors. *Journal of Emerging Trends in Computing and Information Sciences, 3*(6), 814–825.

Index

A
Adaptive control of thought in information foraging model (ACT-IF), 12, 84, 88
Adaptive control of thought-rational model (ACT-R), 84, 88
Advanced V-model, 29
Agile life cycle model, 31–33
 advantage, 32
 construction iterations, 32
 example, 32f
 principles, 31
 product release, 32
 project initiation, 32
 project selection and approval, 31–32
Agile methodology, 42–43
 advantage, 42–43
 extreme programming (XP), 43
Attitudes, 13, 93, 100, 101f

B
Behavior, 13, 15, 53, 70, 88, 92, 93, 94, 95, 96, 97, 100, 101f
Behavioral model, 126, 126f
Beliefs, 13, 95, 96, 100, 101, 101f, 108, 109, 113, 116, 117
 behavioral beliefs, 103, 104f
 control beliefs, 103, 104f
 normative beliefs, 103, 104f

C
CGI Lua, 70
Cognitive walk-throughs, 84–85
 steps involved, 84–85
Composite logical data design (CLDD), 44
Computer-aided software engineering (CASE) toolset, 53, 64

D
Data flow diagrams (DFDs), 44, 52
Decision making, 38, 67, 83, 91, 95, 96, 105, 106, 107, 125, 137
DeLone and McLean's (D&M) IS success model, 15, 15f, 122–125, 138, 139
 information quality, 123
 net benefits, 124
 original model of IS success, 123f, 124–125
 service quality, 123–124
 system quality, 123
 system use, 124
 temporal and causal relation, 125
 updated model, 124f

E
Early Methodology Era, 51
Effective technical and human implementation of computer-based systems (ETHICS), 8, 49–51
 central aspects, 49
 design tools, 51
 purposes, 50
 six-stage design, 50f
Entity life histories (ELHs), 44
Executive process-interactive control (EPIC) model, 84, 87, 87f
Expectation-confirmation theory (ECT), 108
 of IS continuance, 111–112
Expectation-disconfirmation model (EDM), 108, 110f
Expectation-disconfirmation theory (EDT), 108–111
 disconfirmation, 109
 expectations, 109
 performance, 109
External information technology (EIT), 130
Extreme programming (XP), 37, 43

F

First cut data design (DD), 44
First cut programs (PROG), 44
Functionalist paradigm, 2, 3f

G

Goals, operators, methods, and selection rules (GOMS) model, 12, 84, 86

H

Hard thinking, 45
Heuristic evaluation, 85
  basic process of, 86f
Human-computer interaction (HCI), 12, 75, 76, 79, 83, 84, 86, 88, 92
  principles, 11
Hybrid system development life cycles, 37
Hypermedia design model (HDM), 68

I

Incremental life cycle model, 24–26
  example of, 25f
Incremental-type models, 5
Individual impact, 14, 123, 133, 139
Information engineering (IE), 52–53
Information engineering methodology (IEM), 52
Information quality, 123, 125, 126, 127, 132
Information system development life cycle models, 21–22
  agile life cycle model, 31–33
  five phases of, 21
  hybrid system development life cycles, 37
  incremental model, 24–26, see also Incremental life cycle model
  prototyping model, 33–34
  rapid application model (RAD), 29–31, see also Rapid application development (RAD) model
  spiral life cycle model, 26–28
  star life cycle model, 35–36
  usability engineering life cycle, 35
  V life cycle model, 28–29
  waterfall model, 22–24, see also Waterfall life cycle model
Information system developmental methodologies (ISDMs), 6–9, 41
  agile methodology, 42–43
  categorization of, 57, 58t

ETHICS methodology, 49–51
information engineering (IE), 52–53
information systems work and analysis of changes (ISAC), 55
Jackson systems development (JSD), 53–54
multiview methodology, 56–57, 56f
STRADIS methodology, 51–52
structured systems analysis and design methodology (SSADM), 43–45
systems methodology (SSM), 45–47
traditional methodologies, 6
traditional versus agile development, 7f
types of, 8t
user-centered development methodology, 47–49, see also User-centered design
Information systems (IS), 1, 121
  and analysis of changes (ISAC), 55
  Delone and McLean's IS success model, 122–125 see also DeLone and McLean's (D&M) IS success model
  different levels of research, 16
  impact measurement model, 16, 132–134
  models for success assessment, 14–16, 121–122
  Seddon's model, 126–130, see also Seddon's model
  strategic information systems planning (SISP) effectiveness, 134–137, see also Strategic information system planning (SISP)
  success measurement research, 139
  3D model of information systems success, 130–132
  work system method (WSM), 138
Information technology (IT), 1, 58, 91, 121, 132
Initial Operational Capability (IOC), 27
Innovation diffusion theory (IDT), 107–108
  communication channels, role of, 107
  compatibility, 108
  complexity, 108
  external features, 108
  internal features, 108
  relative advantage, 108
Innovation-decision process, 107, 109f
Intention, 13, 16, 41, 79, 95, 100, 101f, 103, 112, 115, 116
Interactionist approach, 3
Internet commerce development methodology (ICDM), 72–74
  implementation and evolution, 73
  logical functional requirements, 73

Index 143

strategy, 72–73
SWOT analysis, 72–73
Web-based systems, perspectives, 74t
Iterative and incremental development model (IIDM), 26

J

Jackson structured programming (JSP), 53
Jackson systems development (JSD), 53–54
  stages of, 54f

K

Knowledge, 4, 12, 22, 46, 49, 66, 79, 86, 91, 95, 107, 115, 139
Knowledge management systems (KMS), 106

L

Life cycle architecture (LCA), 27
Life cycle objectives (LCO), 27
Logical data structures (LDS), 44
Logical dialogue outlines (LDOs), 44
Lua scripting language, 70

M

Management information systems (MIS), 70

N

Neohumanist paradigm, 3, 3f

O

Object-oriented hypermedia design methodology (OOHDM), 9, 68–70
  abstract interface design, 69
  conceptual design stage, 68
  four-stage design, 69t
  implementation, 69–70
  navigational design, 68–69
Organizational impact, 14, 15, 123, 125, 130, 133, 134

P

Participative methodology for, 76–79
  Analysis (SA3), 77
  Content Management Systems (CMS) (SA9), 79
  Design (SA4), 77–78
  Functionality Testing (SA1), 76
  Implementation (SA5), 78
  Iteration (SA8), 78–79
  Maintenance (SA6), 78
  for marketing Web sites, 77f
  Planning (SA2), 76–77
  Usability Evaluation (SA0), 76
  User Participation (SA7), 78
Persuasion, 107
Physical design control (PDC), 44
Process outlines (POs), 44
Product backlog, 43
Professional work practice approach, 3
Prototyping model, 33–34, 33f
  evolutionary approach, 34
  experimental approach, 34
  exploratory approach, 34

Q

Quality evaluation models, 13–14, 91–92
  expectation-disconfirmation theory (EDT), 108–111
  innovation diffusion theory (IDT), 107–108
  social influence model, 112–114
  task-technology fit (TTF) model, 104–107
  technology acceptance model (TAM), 92–95
  technology acceptance model 2 (TAM2), 95–97
  theory of planned behavior (TPB), 102–104
  theory of reasoned action (TRA), 100–102
  unified theory of acceptance and use of technology (UTAUT), 114–116
  web of system performance (WOSP), 97–100

R

Radical structuralist paradigm, 2, 3f
Rapid application development (RAD) model, 6, 29–31, 74
  four-stage cycles, 30
  succession of increments, 30f
  three-stage cycles, 30
Relational data analysis/third normal form (RDA/TNF), 44
Relationship management methodology (RMM), 10, 66–68
  construction and testing, 67
  conversion protocol design, 67
  design processes of, 10f
  entity design, 66
  entity-relationship (E-R) design, 66
  hypermedia design method (HDM), 67

Relationship management methodology
  (RMM) (*cont.*)
 m-slices, 67
 navigational design, 67
 relationship data models, 67
 runtime behavior design, 67
 simplified model of, 67*f*
 user interface design, 67

S
Scrum method, 43
Scrum/XP hybrid methods, 43
Seddon's model, 126–130, 138
 behavioral model, 126*f*
 combinations of system and stakeholders, 129*t*
 external impact, 130
 group impact, 128, 130
 IS effectiveness matrix, 127
 IS success model, 127*f*
 stakeholder variable, 128
 system variable, 128
 user satisfaction, 127
Semantic success, 123
SERVQUAL instrument, 123
Social cognitive theory (SCT), 106
Social influence model (SIM), 112–114, 114*f*
 concept, 113
 definition, 113
Social relativist paradigm, 2, 3*f*
Soft systems methodology (SSM), 3, 8, 45–47
 stages, 46*f*
Soft thinking, 45
Speech act–based approach, 3
Spiral life cycle model, 26–28
 and incremental life cycle model, 26
 invariants, 26–27
 summary, 27*f*
Spiral SDLC model, 6
Sprint, 43
Star life cycle model, 35–36, 36*f*
Strategic information system planning (SISP), 121
 alignment, 136
 analysis, 136
 contribution, 137
 cooperation, 137
 definition, 134
 effectiveness, 134–137
 improvement in capabilities, 137
 key success factors, 135
 model for success, 137*f*
 planning approach, 135

planning context, 136
process of, 135*f*
stages of, 135
Structured analysis, design and implementation of information systems (STRADIS), 8, 51–52, 52*f*
Structured systems analysis and design methodology (SSADM), 7, 43–45
 principles of, 45*t*
 stages of, 44
System development life cycle (SDLC), 4–6, 16, 22, 51, 74
 incremental-type models, 5
 waterfall-type model, 4–5, 5*f*
System quality, 15, 123, 125, 126, 127, 132, 138
System-environment interaction
 aspects of, 98*f*
 and goals of WOSP, 99
Systems development paradigms, 2–4

T
Task-technology fit (TTF) model, 104–107
 conceptual model, 106*f*
 individuals, 105
 tasks, 105
 technologies, 105
Technology acceptance model (TAM), 13, 14*f*, 92–95, 138
 model in depth, 94*f*
 outline of, 93*f*
Technology acceptance model 2 (TAM2), 95–97, 96
 cognitive instruments, 95
 compliance, 96
 expert power, 96
 identification, 96
 image, 96
 internalization, 96
 job relevance, 97
 output quality, 97
 perceived ease of use, 97
 result demonstrability, 97
 social influence, 95
 subjective norm, 95
 voluntariness, 95
Theory of planned behavior (TPB), 13, 102–104
 behavioral beliefs, 103, 104*f*
 control beliefs, 103, 104*f*
 model for, 104*f*
 normative beliefs, 103, 104*f*
 perceived behavioral control, 103

Theory of reasoned action (TRA), 13, 100–102
    attitudes, 100, 101f
    behaviors, 100, 101f
    beliefs, 100, 101f
    intentions, 100, 101f
    model for, 102f
3D model of information systems success, 130–132, 131f
    deployment, 131
    development stage, 130–131
    environment, 131
    fundamental aspect of, 132
    implementation, 131
Trade unionist approach, 3

U

Unified theory of acceptance and use of technology (UTAUT), 14, 114–116, 115f
    effort expectancy, 115
    facilitating conditions, 116
    performance expectancy, 115
Usability engineering, 35
Usability engineering life cycle, 35
Usability evaluation models, 11–12, 83
    adaptive control of thought in information foraging model (ACT-IF), 88
    adaptive control of thought-rational model (ACT-R), 88
    cognitive engineering, 83–84, 84f
    cognitive walk-throughs, 84–85
    executive process-interactive control (EPIC) model, 87
    goals, operators, methods, and selection rules (GOMS), 86
    heuristic evaluation, 85–86
User satisfaction, 14, 15, 47, 53, 111, 123, 124, 126, 127, 133, 138, 139
User-centered design (UCD), 47–49
    principles of, 48t

V

V life cycle model (V-Model), 5, 28–29, 28f

W

Waterfall life cycle model, 22–24
    analysis and coding, 23
    example of, 24f
    methodology, 74
    principles for software development, 23
    type model, 4–5, 5f
Web Engineering, 70–72
    levels of Web development, 71f
    stages of development, 71–72
Web information system development methodology (WISDM), 10, 74–76
    human-computer interaction (HCI), 75
    information analysis, 75
    matrix of, 75f
    organizational analysis, 75
    technical design, 75
    user interface (UI) design, 75
    work design, 75
Web of system performance (WOSP), 97–100
    boundary, 98
    central concept, 97–98
    effectors, 98
    goals of, 98–99
    internal structure, 98
    receptors, 98
    virtual environment Second Life, 99–100
Web site design method, 65–66
    conceptual design, 65
    implementation design, 66
    mission statement specification, 65
    user modeling, 65
Web site developmental methodologies (WSDM), 9–11, 63
    developing Web sites, participative methodology for, 76–79
    Internet commerce development methodology (ICDM), 72–74
    model of, 64f
    object-oriented hypermedia design methodology (OOHDM), 68–70
    relationship management methodology (RMM), 66–68
    W3DT methodology, 63–64
    Web Engineering, 70–72
    Web information system development methodology (WISDM), 74–76
    web site design method, 65–66
WebDesigner, 64
Work system method (WSM) of IS success measurement, 138
Workshop on Web Engineering, 9
World Wide Web, 63
    based hypermedia applications, 63
    Design Technique (W3DT), 63–64

MIX
Papier aus verantwortungsvollen Quellen
Paper from responsible sources
FSC® C105338

If you have any concerns about our products,
you can contact us on
ProductSafety@springernature.com

In case Publisher is established outside the EU,
the EU authorized representative is:
**Springer Nature Customer Service Center GmbH
Europaplatz 3, 69115 Heidelberg, Germany**

Printed by Libri Plureos GmbH
in Hamburg, Germany